THE

ESSENTIALS OF LOGIC

By Dr. Bernard Bosanquet

THE PHILOSOPHICAL THEORY OF THE STATE

THE

ESSENTIALS OF LOGIC

BEING

TEN LECTURES ON JUDGMENT AND INFERENCE

BY

BERNARD BOSANQUET

FORMERLY FELLOW OF UNIVERSITY COLLEGE, OXFORD

LONDON

MACMILLAN & CO LTD

NEW YORK · ST MARTIN'S PRESS

1960

MACMILLAN AND COMPANY LIMITED
London Bombay Calcutta Madras Melbourne

THE MACMILLAN COMPANY OF CANADA LIMITED
Toronto

ST MARTIN'S PRESS INC
New York

PRINTED IN GREAT BRITAIN

PREFACE

In this course of lectures I have attempted to carry out, under the freer conditions of the University Extension system, a purpose conceived many years ago at Oxford. It was suggested to me by the answer of a friend, engaged like myself from time to time in teaching elementary Logic, to the question which I put to him, "What do you aim at in teaching Logic to beginners? What do you think can reasonably be hoped for?" "If the men could learn what an Inference is, it would be something," was the reply.

The course of lectures which I now publish was projected in the spirit thus indicated. Though only the two last discourses deal explicitly with Inference, yet those which precede them contribute, I hope, no less essentially, to explain the nature of that single development which in some stages we call Judgment, and in others Inference. So far as I could see, the attempt to go to the heart of the subject, however imperfectly executed, was appreciated by the students, and was rewarded with a serious attention which would not have been commanded by the trivialities of formal Logic, although more entertaining and less abstruse.

The details of traditional terminology may be found in Jevons's *Elementary Lessons in Logic* (Macmillan). Those who desire to pursue the study more in the sense of the present work, may be referred above all to Bradley's *Principles of Logic*, and also to Lotze's *Logic* (E. Tr.), and to Sigwart's great work on Logic, the English translation of which, just completed, opens a storehouse of knowledge and robust good sense to the English student. My own larger *Logic* expresses *in extenso* the views which these lectures set out in a shorter form.

I hope it will be admitted by my critics that this experiment, whether successful or unsuccessful, was worth making, and that except in the University Extension system, it could not easily have been made.

BERNARD BOSANQUET.

London, January 1895.

CONTENTS

LECTURE I

THE PROBLEM OF LOGIC

LECTURE II

JUDGMENT AS THE CONSCIOUSNESS OF A WORLD

LECTURE III

THE RELATION OF LOGIC TO KNOWLEDGE

LECTURE IV

TYPES OF JUDGMENT, AND THE GENERAL CONDITIONS INVOLVED IN ASSERTION

LECTURE V

THE PROPOSITION AND THE NAME

LECTURE VI

PARTS OF THE JUDGMENT, AND ITS UNITY

LECTURE VII

THE CATEGORICAL AND THE HYPOTHETICAL JUDGMENTS

LECTURE VIII

NEGATION, AND OPPOSITION OF JUDGMENTS

LECTURE IX

INFERENCE AND THE SYLLOGISTIC FORMS

LECTURE X

INDUCTION, DEDUCTION, AND CAUSATION

LECTURE I

THE PROBLEM OF LOGIC

1. THERE is no science more difficult than that on which Difficulty we are entering in these lectures. It is worth while to of the discuss the nature of this difficulty. It is a question of science. interest rather than of intricacy. All sciences have, perhaps, much the same possibilities of broad theory and subtle analysis. But Logic stands alone in the difficulty with which the student sustains his persuasion that its point of view is worth applying.

In most other sciences, even in the philosophical sciences, there is a continual stimulus to sense-perception, to curiosity, to human interest. The learner is called upon to dissect animals or plants, to undertake delicate manipulations with beautifully contrived instruments, to acquaint himself with the history of nations, with the genesis of worlds, with strange and novel speculations upon the nature of space, or with the industry and well-being of various classes among mankind at the present day. And these elements of novelty, these stimulations of sense-perception or of practical interest, carry us forward imperceptibly, and sustain our

B

eagerness to analyse and combine in theoretic completeness the novel matter thus constantly impinging upon us.

In Philosophy, and more especially in Logic, we can promise little or nothing of this kind. The teacher of Philosophy, from Socrates downwards, has talked about common things, things already familiar to his hearers. And although he calls upon them to think of these things in a peculiar way, and from an unaccustomed point of view, yet it is likely to be felt that he is demanding a new effort, without supplying a new interest. And it is a common experience, that after a time the mind rebels against this artificial attitude, which fatigues without instructing, if we have accustomed ourselves to understand by instruction the accumulation of new sense-perceptions and the extension of historical or scientific vision over a wider superficial area.

Now this I cannot help, and I will not disguise. In Philosophy, and in Logic above all, it must be so. The whole point and meaning of the study is that in it we re-traverse familiar ground, and survey it by unfamiliar processes. We do not, except accidentally, so much as widen our mental horizon. For those who care to understand, to trace the connecting principles and functions that permeate our intellectual world, there is indeed an interest of a peculiar kind. But even experienced students will occasionally feel the strain of attending to difficult distinctions, entirely without the excitement of novelty in sense-perception or of a practical bearing upon human life. It is this that makes Logic probably the hardest of all the sciences.

2. We cannot hope to vanquish this difficulty unless we The
face it boldly from the first. There are in the old-fashioned problem
stated.
Logic-books tricks and puzzles, fallacies and repartees, which
can in some degree be made amusing ; but of these I do
not intend to speak. The course by which alone I can hope
honestly to awaken a true logical interest among any who
may be quite unfamiliar with the subject, is to approach the
matter descriptively, and try to set before you fully and
fairly what the problem is which the process of knowledge
has to meet. And then it may be possible to claim a genuine
theoretical curiosity—none the less genuine that it may be
tinged with a sympathy for man's common birthright of
intelligence—for the detailed explanation of the means by
which this problem is solved from day to day. Such an
explanation is the science of Logic.

The problem may be thus introduced. Several of those
present have, I believe, attended a previous course of
lectures on Psychology. They have learned, I presume,
to think of the mind as the course of consciousness, a
continuous connected presentation, more or less emphasising
within it various images, and groups of images and ideas,
which may be roughly said to act and re-act upon each other,
to cohere in systems, and to give rise to the perception of
self. This course of consciousness, including certain latent
elements, the existence of which it is necessary to assume,
is an individual mind, attached to a particular body, and so
far as we know, not separable from the actions and affections
of that body. What is the connection between such a
course of consciousness in any individual, and the world as
that individual knows and wills it ? This is the point at

which Psychology passes into Logic. Psychology treats of the course of ideas and feelings; Logic of the mental construction of reality. How does the course of my private ideas and feelings contain in it, for me, a world of things and persons which are *not merely in my mind?*

World as Idea.

3. Schopenhauer called his great work, *The World as Will and Idea.*[1] Leaving out Will for the moment, let us consider the world "as Idea."

"'The world is my idea;'[2] this is a truth which holds good for everything that lives and knows, though man alone can bring it into reflective and abstract consciousness. If he really does this, he has attained to philosophical wisdom. It then becomes clear and certain to him that what he knows is not a sun and an earth, but only an eye that sees a sun, a hand that feels an earth; that the world which surrounds him is there only as an idea, *i. e.* only in relation to something else, the consciousness which is himself. If any truth can be asserted *a priori*, it is this; for it is the expression of the most general form of all possible and thinkable experience: a form which is more general than time, space, or causality, for they all pre-suppose it.

* * * * * *

"No truth, therefore, is more certain, more independent of all others, and less in need of proof than this, that all that exists for knowledge, and, therefore, this whole world, is only object in relation to subject, perception of a perceiver, in a word, idea. This is obviously true of the past and the future, as well as of the present, of what is farthest off, as of

---

[1] E. Tr. (Trübner, 1883).
[2] Schopenhauer, *op. cit.*, beginning.

what is near ; for it is true of time and space themselves, in which alone these distinctions arise. All that in any way belongs or can belong to the world is inevitably thus conditioned through the subject and exists only for the subject. The world is idea."

The world, then, for each of us, exists in the medium of our mind. It is a sort of building, of which the materials are our ideas and perceptions.

4. So much for "idea." What do we mean by "world"? *The* A succession of images passing before us, or rather making *"world."* up our consciousness, like a dream, is not a world. The term is very expressive ; it is a favourite word in Shakespeare. When the courtier says—

> " Hereafter, in a better world than this,
> I shall desire more love and knowledge of you."

he does not mean, as I used to think, "in heaven " ; he means in a better condition of social affairs. In "mad world, mad kings, mad composition," the term means more especially the set of political and family connections within which extraordinary reversals of behaviour have just taken place. Often we use the expression, with a qualifying epithet, to indicate some particular sphere of connected action, "the ecclesiastical world," "the political world," and so forth. Always there seems to be implied the notion of a set of things or persons bound together by some common quality which enables them to act upon each other, and to constitute what is technically termed a " whole." *The* " world " *par excellence*, then, ought to mean the one connected set of things and persons which we all recognise and refer to as the same, and as including ourselves along with all who use the word in the same sense.

Then the "world as idea" means no less than this, that the system of things and persons which surrounds all of us, and which each of us speaks of and refers to as the same for every one, exists for each of us as something built up in his own mind—the mind attached to his own body—and out of the material of his own mind.

The animal's world.

5. Let us illustrate this building up by thinking of the world, our surroundings, as an animal must be aware of it. The lowest beginnings of sight, for example, give no colour and no shape. An animal in this stage can, probably, only just take warning if a dark object comes between him and the light. Therefore he cannot have the ordered visual image of space definitely stretching away all round him, which is the primary basis of our idea of a world. He can move, no doubt, but there is nothing to make us suppose that he records and co-ordinates the results of his movements into anything like that permanent order of objects which must be constructed in some way by a human being even though born blind. Succession, we might say, is much more powerful with animals than co-existence; but we should have to guard ourselves against supposing that this was what we mean by succession, that is, a process definitely recognised as in time, with a connection of some reasonable kind between its phases. For the most part with animals out of sight is out of mind; if so, the present is not interpreted, enlarged, and arranged with reference to what is not present in time or space by them as it is by us. And therefore the consciousness of a single system of things,

permanent, and distinct from the momentary presentations of the senses, cannot, in all probability, grow up for them. If so, they have no real world, but only a dream world,[1] *i. e.* a world not contrasted with the stream of presentation, nor taken as the common theatre of all actions and events. This difference between the world of an animal and that of a human being, is a rough measure of what man does by mental or intellectual construction in making his world.

6. We have now got the idea of a "world," as a system The world of things and persons connected together, taken to be the as object-ive. same for oneself at different times and for different minds at the same time, yet existing, for oneself, in the medium of one's individual consciousness.

We see at once that we cannot stop here. We have really got a contradiction. If the parts of our world are connected with each other, they are not merely dependent upon us, that is, upon the changes of our consciousness. And we all take them to be independent of us, in the sense that we do not suppose the presence or absence of our perception to make any difference to the world except by the continuance or cessation of our perception of it or of its parts. This is the state of mind in which we practically live, philosophers and all. I do not really take notice of any difference in mode of existence between the wall in front of me, which I see, and the wall behind me, which I

---

[1] The character of the sensory powers, which are strongest in many animals, contributes to this conclusion. Mr. F. H. Bradley is sure that his dog's system of logic, if he had one, would run, " What exists smells ; what does not smell is nothing." The sense of smell can scarcely give rise to the idea of a world of objects. It has hardly any capacity of structural discernment.

do not see. While you are in this lecture-hall, if you think of your rooms at home, you think of them as they look, that is, as they would look if you were there to see them. How else, indeed, could you think of them? This is practically necessary, and therefore, for practical purposes, true.

But if you take it as a theory, omitting the hypothetical factor, "if I was there to see," you go wrong. You then treat your world as being, outside your consciousness, the same that it is inside your consciousness, without allowing for the withdrawal of your consciousness. You are then on the way to think that the world, *as you see, hear, and feel it*, is outside your mind, and that the sight, hearing, feeling, and the ideas born of them, are inside your mind as a sort of faint and imperfect *copy* of the world which you then call "external," *in the sense of outside the mind.*

Common sense.

i. The first position was that of common sense. The second is that of common-sense theory. Common sense is quite justified. It says, "Things affect each other, but the mere presence and absence of our perception does not affect them." For practical purposes we must treat them as being, when unapprehended by our minds, just the same as when apprehended by our minds. This is the first idea or rather postulate—for it is not a theoretical idea—of objectivity. Objective = "independent of our consciousness for practical purposes."

Common-sense theory.

ii. In describing the second position as that of common-sense theory I do not refer to the doctrine of any regular school of philosophers. There was a Scotch school of philosophy—the school of Reid in the eighteenth century—commonly called the common-sense school. I will say

below how I think this school was related to the position
which I am now describing. But my present purpose is to
hit off the simple theory of reality which common-sense
people make for themselves when they reflect. Now this
theory, in which we all live except when we make a special
effort, accepts the distinction between things and the mind.
For example, it defines truth as the conformity of ideas to
objects. That means something of this kind : the ideas are
inside our heads, and the objects are outside our heads.
If we are to have knowledge, the objects have to be represented inside our heads, and they get in through the senses.
And then you have two similar forms of the world, one
outside our heads, which is real, and another like it but less
perfect and without solidity or causal power, inside our
heads, which is ideal or mental. This is what I call the
common-sense theory of the Objective. Like common sense,
it assumes that there is a world which the withdrawal of our
individual consciousness does not affect, but which persists
and acts all the same. Unlike common sense, it lays down
an assertion as to the nature of this world, viz. that it is,
apart from our consciousness, the same as it is for our consciousness. The world in consciousness, it assumes, is
subjective, the world out of consciousness is objective, and
the former is an imperfect copy of the latter in a feebler
material.

The schools of common-sense philosophy, such as are
represented by Locke and Reid, are not quite so simple-
minded as the reflection of ordinary common sense, because
every systematic thinker sees at once that the question stares
him in the face, "If the world outside the mind is copied

by the world inside the mind, how can we ever know whether the copy conforms to the original?" We are by the hypo-thesis inside the mind; whatever has passed through the senses is inside the mind. We cannot as at present advised get at anything outside the senses or outside the mind. In face of this question, the common-sense philosophies have two courses open. They may start from the idea of things outside the mind, but admit that in passing through the senses the things are in some partial respects transformed—as for instance, that they acquire colour, sound, and smell in passing through the senses—this is what Locke says. Or again, still starting from the idea of things outside the mind, they may simply assert that perception is of such a nature that it gives us things as they really are. The former was the view of Locke, the latter that of Reid. This latter view obviously might pass into the most extreme idealism, and its interpretation, if it does not so pass, is exceedingly difficult.

But whatever may have been the view of the historical "common-sense school,"[1] the common-sense theory which we all make for ourselves involves a separation between the mind and reality. The objective world is the world as inde-pendent of mind, and independent of mind means existing and acting outside mind, exactly, or almost exactly, as it seems to exist and act before the mind.

Now this is an absolute *cul-de-sac*. If the objective is that which is outside perception, the objective is out of our reach, and the world of our perception can never be objec-tive. This is the pass to which we are brought by taking

[1] See Seth, *Scottish Philosophy* (Blackwood, 1885).

common sense as the guide of theory and not as its material.

iii. There is no way out but by retracing our steps, and avoiding a false turn which we took in passing from common sense to common-sense theory.   It was quite true that the world is unaffected by the withdrawal of my individual perception and consciousness (except in so far as I acted *qua* bodily thing in the world) ; but it does not follow from this that *if* it becomes the object of a consciousness in me, it can be so otherwise than as presented within that consciousness. We must distinguish between the idea that the objective is outside consciousness and therefore not in consciousness, and the idea that the objective can be in the individual consciousness, but identified with something beyond the individual consciousness.   It may be that consciousness is capable of containing a world, not as a copy of a ready-made original, but as something which it makes for itself by a necessary process, and which refers beyond this finite and momentary consciousness.

Philosophical theory.

According to these ideas, the objective is, shortly stated, whatever we are obliged to think.   This, though it is *in* our thought, is not considered merely *as* our thought, or as a train of images or whole of presentation in our minds.   That is an artificial point of view, the point of view of psychology, and we must carefully avoid starting from it.   But knowledge refers beyond its mental self, and has no limitation in time or in kind except its own necessity.   Thus, I am forced to think, by a certain context of ideas and perceptions, that there is now a fire burning in my study at home.   This judgment is not barred by the fact that my mind, as a

function attached to my body, is here three miles away.   The
thought is objective for me, so long as I am obliged to think
it.   My presence in or absence from the room where the fire
is burning has no effect on the question, except as it fur-
nishes me with evidence one way or the other.   Not only
absence in space is no obstacle, but succession in time is no
obstacle.   My thought, which *is* here and now, refers con-
fidently to what has happened in long intervals of time, if
the necessity of consistency obliges it to do so.   Thus if I
go back to my room and find the fire out and the room very
cold, I infer without hesitation to certain acts and events
which are needed to explain this state of things.   And inter-
pretations or explanations of this kind make up my world,
which is for me in my thought, but is presented as more than
my thought, and cannot be a world at all unless it is more
than in my thought.   It is in as far as my thought constructs and presents a world which is more than my momentary psychical state, that my thought, and the world as
presented to me in it, is objective.   The world is not a set
of my ideas, but it is a set of objects and relations of which
I frame an idea, and the existence of which has no meaning
for me except as presented in the idea which I frame.   We
are not to think of (i) Ideas, and (ii) Things which they
represent ;   the ideas, taken as parts of a world, *are* the
things.

We begin to see, then, how the nature of knowledge
meets the puzzle which I stated above.   How, I asked, can
a connected " world," whose parts act on one another quite
independently of my perception, be in my individual mind ?
I answer that it does not follow, because the world *is for me*

only in my presentation, that my presentation is the only thing which goes on in the world. "What I am obliged to think" may represent a real development depending on laws and a system which is not confined to my individual course of consciousness. The "objective" in this sense is for Logic an assumption, or rather a fact to be analysed. We do not attempt to prove its existence, except in the sense of calling attention to its nature in detail. It will be seen that "outside the mind" ceases, on this view of objectivity, to have meaning as regards anything that can be related to us. "Outside" is a relation of bodies to one another; but everything, about which we can so much as ask a question, is so far inside the mind, *i. e.* given in its continuum of presentation or idea.

I will recapitulate the three conceptions of the "objective."

(1) According to practical "common sense" the objective is independent of our consciousness in the sense that the presence or absence of our consciousness makes no difference to the operation of things upon each other.

(2) According to "common-sense theory" the objective is independent of our consciousness in the sense that the presence or absence of our consciousness makes no difference in the mode of being of things (viz. that the world in consciousness approaches objectivity by resembling or reproducing a similar and quite objective world outside consciousness).

(3) According to philosophical theory the objective is independent of our consciousness in the sense that it is what we are constrained to think in order to make our consciousness consistent with itself. " What we are constrained to

think " is not confined, in its *reference*, to our thought, or to thought at all.

Our separate worlds.

7. Thus, for the purposes of Logic, we must turn our usual ideas upside down. We must try to imagine something of this kind. We have all seen a circular panorama. Each one of us, we must think, is shut up alone inside such a panorama, which is movable and flexible, and follows him wherever he goes. The things and persons depicted in it move and act upon one another ; but all this is in the panorama, and not beyond it. The individual cannot get outside this encircling scenery, and no one else can get inside it. Apart from it, prior to it, we have no self ; it is indeed the stuff of which oneself is made. Is every one's panorama exactly the same? No, they are not exactly the same. They are formed round different centres, each person differing from all the others by individual qualities, and by his position towards the points and processes which determine his picture. For—and here is the remarkable point—every one of us has painted for himself the picture within which he is shut up, and he is perpetually painting and re-painting it, not by copying from some original, but by arranging and completing confused images and tints that are always appearing magically on his canvas. Now this magical panorama, from which the individual cannot escape, and the laws of which are the laws of his experience, is simply his own mind regarded as a content or a world. His own body and mind, regarded as things, are within the panorama, just as other people's bodies and minds are. The whole world, for each of us, *is* our course of consciousness, in so far as this is regarded as a system of objects which we are obliged to

think. Not, in so far as it really *is* a system, for an onlooker, say for a psychologist. For no doubt every child's mind, and every animal's mind, *is* a working system of presentations, which a psychologist may study and analyse from without. Consciousness is consciousness of a world only in so far as it *presents* a system, a whole of objects, acting on one another, and therefore independent of the presence or absence of the consciousness which presents them.

I take another very rough metaphor to explain this curious contrast between my mind as a working system, observable from without, and belonging to my individual body—distinguishable from the thirty or forty quite different minds belonging to the thirty or forty persons in this room—and my mind as a continuum of presentations which includes, as objects, itself, and all the other minds in the room, and the whole world so far as I have any conscious relation to it whatever.

All of us are familiar with the appearance of a microscope ready adjusted for use, with its little lamp, its mirror and illuminating apparatus under the stage, with a specimen on the stage under the object-glass, its object-glass and its eye-piece. Any one who understands the working of a microscope finds this a most suggestive spectacle. He follows in his imagination the light as it comes from the lamp to the mirror, through the illuminating lenses, through the transparent specimen, through perhaps a dozen lenses arranged as an object-glass within an inch of distance, through the eye-piece and into the observer's eye. Give him the parts, lenses, prisms, and mirrors into his hands, and he will test them all, and tell you exactly how they work. This scientific onlooker may be compared to the psychologist looking at another man's mind. He sees it as a thing among other things, a working system of parts.

But there is one thing that the mere onlooker cannot see. He cannot see the object. That can only be seen by look-ing through the tube. And every one has felt, I should think, the magical transformation, suggestive of looking through another man's eye and mind, which occurs when you put your eye to the eye-piece of an optical instrument. The outside world of other objects, the tube, the stage, the mirror, the bystanders, the external light, all disappear, and you see nothing but the field of vision and whatever dis-tinctly pictured structure may be displayed within it. The observer who looks through the tube may be compared with each one of us as he contemplates his own world of know-ledge and perception. This is a thing that no one else can ever do.

The metaphor, indeed, breaks down, in so far as each of us is able to observe the history and character of his own mind as an object within the field of presentation which is before his mind. Of course such a metaphor must break down at some point. But it remains true that the mind, while directly observing its field of objects, cannot observe its own peculiarities, and when turned, as we say, upon itself, is still observing only a part of itself. It remains true that my mind contains the whole presented world for me, and is merely one among thousands of similar mind-things for you.

Thus, I repeat, the world for each of us is our course of consciousness, looked at in that way in which it presents a systematic, organised picture of inter-acting objects, not in that way in which it is a stream of ideas and feelings, taking place in our several heads. In the former point of view it is the world as our idea; in the latter point of view it is simply the consciousness attached to our body. We might soon puzzle ourselves with the contradictions which arise if we fail to distinguish these points of view. In one sense my mind is in my head, in the other sense my head is in my mind. In the one sense I am in space, in the other sense space is in me. Just so, however rough the metaphor, from one point of view the microscope is one among a host of things seen from the outside; from the other point of view all that we see is in the microscope, which is itself not seen at all.

It is in this latter sense that our mental equipment is looked at, when it is regarded as knowledge; and it is in this sense that it forms a panorama which absolutely shuts in every one of us into his own circle of ideas. (It is not implied, we should carefully observe, that his ideas or experience are in any way secondary to his self, or separable from it, or an adjective of it.) Then how does it happen that our separate worlds, the panoramas which we construct, do not contradict one another?

The answer is, that they *correspond*. It is this conception from which we must start in Logic. We must learn to regard our separate worlds of knowledge as something constructed by definite processes, and corresponding to each other in consequence of the common nature of these processes. We know that we begin apart. We begin in fact, though not conscious of our limits, with feelings and fancies and unorganised experiences which give us little or no common ground and power of co-operation with other people. But as the constructive process advances, the correspondence between our worlds is widened and deepened, and the greater proportion of what we are obliged to think is in harmony with what other people are obliged to think. Now of course this would not be so unless reality, the whole actual system in which we find ourselves, were self-consistent. But more than that, it would not be so unless the nature of intelligence were the same in every mind. It is this common nature of intelligence, together with its differentiated adaptations to reality, that we have to deal with in Logic.

Thus the separate worlds, in which we are all shut up, must be considered as corresponding so far as they are objective, that is, so far as they approach what we are ultimately obliged to think. I say "corresponding," because that is the term which expresses the relation between systems which represent the same thing by the same rules, but with different starting-points. Drawings in perspective of the same building from different points of view are such corresponding systems; the parts represented answer each to each, but the same part is near or large in one drawing, and distant and small in another; not, however, by chance, but as a definite consequence of the same laws. Our separate worlds may be compared to such drawings: the things in them are identified by their relations and functions, so that we can understand each other, *i. e.* make identical references, though my drawing be taken from the east, and yours from the west. The things do not look quite the same in our different worlds; besides being taken from different standpoints, both drawings are imperfect and incorrect. But so long as we can make out the correspondence, we have a basis for co-operation and for discussion. Logic shows us the principles and processes by which, under the given influences, these drawings are constructed.

8. If we merely hold to the doctrine of separate worlds, *Subjective Idealism.* without insisting upon their correspondence with each other and with reality, we fall back into the position of subjective idealism, which is a natural completion of common-sense theory, when, instead of turning round to retrace its path, it runs deeper into the *cul-de-sac.* It is a very obvious reflection, that each of us is shut up within his own mind, and much easier to grasp than the reason for assuming a real system which appears differently, though correspondingly, in the centres of consciousness which are ourselves. We cannot get at anything but in terms of consciousness; how can we justify the assumption that our consciousness of a world of objects is rooted in reality, *e. g.* that objects may rightly be treated as persisting and inter-acting when our personal consciousness is withdrawn? And if we once doubt this, then why should we assume that our ideas need be or tend to be consistent with themselves and each other, as for the time they apparently are?

Subjective Idealism necessarily arises if the common-sense theory of two worlds, the real outside the mind, and the ideal, copying it, within the mind, is pushed to its conclusion. The real, outside the mind, being inaccessible, falls away. The arguments of this Idealism, as Hume said, "admit of no answer and produce no conviction."[1] But I

[1] Vol. iv. p. 176 (ed. of 1854), *Inquiry concerning Human Understanding*, sect. 12

mention the idea, because I do not think that any one can really understand the problem of Logic, or indeed of science in general, without having thoroughly thought himself into the difficulty of Subjective Idealism. It is necessary to be wholly dissatisfied with common-sense theory, and with the notion of a ready-made world set up for us to copy in the mind, before the logical analysis of intellectual construction can have interest or meaning for us. And to produce this dissatisfaction is the value of Subjective Idealism.

LECTURE II

"JUDGMENT" AS THE CONSCIOUSNESS OF A WORLD

1. THE last lecture was devoted to explaining the distinction between the stream of presentations and the world
as it is for knowledge. I ended by calling attention to the
theory known as "Subjective Idealism." This, I said, has
the merit of forcing upon us the question, "How do we get
from mind to reality? How do we get from subjective to
objective?" For we have always to remember that our
knowledge *is* within consciousness, though it may *refer*
outside it. Defect of Subjective Idealism.

On the other hand, Subjective Idealism has the *defect* of
confounding the very distinction which we took so much
trouble to make plain. Its essence lies in ascribing to the
world of knowledge properties which are only true of the
stream of presentation. It is quite true that the actual
presentations of this room, which each of us has in his head
at this moment, are all different from each other, and
different from any which we have had before, and shall ever
have again. Every minute, every second, they differ; they
are perishing existences, wholly mental, and each of them
when past is irrecoverably gone. That is the property of a
presentation within the course of consciousness. It is a
particular perishing existence.

But Subjective Idealism says, "Because these mental existences are particular perishing existences, and all knowledge consists in them as its medium, therefore the object of knowledge is nothing beyond these mental facts, and is not rooted in a permanent system[1] independent of our mental connections." Here we must check the inference, and reply, "No, it does not follow. The presentations which themselves come and go may refer to something in common, and through them all we may become aware of something that is not wholly in any of them." In other words, there is in Knowledge no passage *from* subjective to objective, but only a development of the objective.

The world as *Knowledge*. 2. Therefore we say, coming closer to our subject, that "*Knowledge* is the medium in which our world, *as an interrelated whole*,[2] exists for us." This is more than saying that it exists in mind or presentation, because the mere course of consciousness need not amount to Knowledge. A world, that is, a system of things acting on one another, could not exist merely in the course of our ideas. But *Knowledge*, we said, is the mental construction of reality. It consists of what we are obliged to assert in thought, and because we are all obliged to think assertorily according to the same methods, the results of our thinking form corresponding systems—systems that correspond alike to each other and to reality. (I may be asked, does not this agreement of

---

[1] Our estimate of Berkeley's view must depend on the degree in which we judge him to have identified the Deity with, or separated Him from, a permanent and universal system. The statement in the text applies fairly to Hume.

[2] The words italicised make a reservation in favour of feeling, which has its own form of reality, but is not relational.

our knowledge depend on the agreement of the physical
stimuli supplied to us by nature, as well as on the homo-
geneousness of our intelligences? The answer is, that these
stimuli, or nature, have no priority in Knowledge. Their
identity is merely a case or consequence of the identity of
our experience as a whole. We are regarding nature as a
system developed in experience, not as an unknown somewhat behind it. To suppose that solid or extended existence
somehow comes before and accounts for everything else, is
a form of the common-sense theory we have dismissed.
Knowledge and Truth have their limitations as forms of
Reality, but an appeal to solidity or extension will not
furnish the required supplementation.)

3. All that we have been saying about Knowledge is *Know-*
summed up in the sentence, "Knowledge is a judgment, *the form of*
an affirmation." We need not trouble ourselves yet about *Judgment.*
negation. We all know what affirmative assertion is, and
it is near enough for the present to say that all knowledge
is judgment in the sense of affirmative assertion.

I will explain how we sum up all we have said of knowledge by calling it a judgment.

Judgment or affirmation always implies three properties,
though they are not always recognised.

It is (a) necessary, (β) universal, and (γ) constructive.

(a) Judgment is necessary. In saying this, we express all *Judgment*
that we said about the objectivity of the world in know- *necessary.*
ledge. "Objective" meant, we concluded, what we are
obliged to think. And judgment is necessary, because it
expresses what we are obliged to think; obliged, that is,
not as we are obliged to feel pain, as an unexplained and

isolated fact, but obliged by a necessity operative within the movement of our consciousness, though not, of course, theoretically recognised as necessity in common thinking. Thus, in the simplest phases of Judgment, necessity does begin to approach the kind of necessity by which we feel pain or are visited by persistent irrational associations.

We can trace an explicit sense of necessity in any scientific matter, or in any doubtful and complex matters in which we are aware of our own reflections. We constantly hear and read such phrases as, "I am unable to resist the conclusion"; "I am forced to believe"; "I am driven to think"; "I have no alternative but to suppose." These are every-day phrases in controversy and in theoretical discussion. And what they all mean is just what was insisted on in the last lecture; the objective or real for us is what we are obliged to think. Given our perceptive state and our mental equipment, the judgment follows.

In trivial or simple judgments this necessity is harder to observe within consciousness, and approaches more and more to the mere constraint exercised upon us by physical reality. In a judgment of mere sensuous comparison, such as a "colour-match," the necessity is not that of an intellectual system, but almost that of a feeling which we cannot dispel. The chief intellectual labour is here negative, and consists in precautions to remove all disturbing influences, both mental and material, so as to let the perception operate freely on the mind. But yet here *is* necessity; we never for a moment think that we can modify the result; our aim is simply to distinguish from all others the particular strand of necessity by which we desire to be guided.

It is easy for an observer to detect intellectual necessity in judgment, even where the judging subject is wholly un-reflective. If you contradict an obvious judgment made by an uneducated man, he will no doubt be quite unable to point out the intellectual necessity which constrains him to it, *i. e.* to argue in support of it ; but he will be bewildered and probably indignant, which shows that, unknown to him-self, his whole intellectual existence is really impeached by impeachment of a necessary conclusion from it. Many people cannot see the difference between impeaching their argument and impeaching their veracity ; and this confusion arises, I presume, from a just feeling that their whole mind is on its trial in the one case as in the other, although they do not distinguish between the forms of its action which are concerned. We are told, indeed, in formal logic, that ordinary statements of fact do not claim necessity ; but this merely arises from confining necessity to explicit necessity expressed in a special grammatical form.

But, it may be objected, we do not always feel that every trivial judgment emanates from and so implicates our whole mental constitution and equipment. If I say to a friend, " I saw you at Charing Cross yesterday," and he says, " No, you could not, for I was out of town," then, unless I was very certain indeed, I should admit having made a mistake, and think no more about the matter. That only means, (1) that the unity of the mind is not thoroughly complete— there are many more or less detached systems in the mind, and one of them may not be very deeply inwrought in the whole intellectual frame ; and (2) the necessity of thought may itself modify the certainty of the fact, *e. g.* I know that a mistake of identity is quite a common thing, and this knowledge co-operates with my friend's denial.

But in any perceptive judgment, however unimportant its immediate content, if it is clear and persistent, a contradiction is a most serious thing. There is a well-known form of bewilderment connected with the judgment of direction; if you forget or do not know of a turn that you have taken, and come out, for example, on familiar ground from the North when you think you are coming on it from the South, so that objects have the reverse position of what you expected, then, supposing that you cannot explain the contradiction, the result is sometimes a very grave perplexity; some men are quite unhinged by it for the moment, and a psychologist in France[1] has given it a new name, "Vertigo of Direction." This again shows how your whole intellectual nature is staked upon the most trifling perception, and if you seem to be forced to a flat contradiction even in the simplest judgment you are almost "beside yourself."

Judgment universal. (β) Judgment is universal. There are different senses of "universal" as of "necessary." We are now speaking only in the widest sense, in which universality is a property of all judgment whatever. If we assume that all our intellectual natures are the same, then to be universal is a mere consequence of being necessary. I not only feel that my judgment is inevitable for me, but I never think of doubting that, given the same materials, it is obligatory for every other intelligent being. If some one disagrees with a judgment of mine, I try to put the case before him as it is in my mind. And I am absolutely sure that if I could do so, he

[1] M. Binet. See *Mind*, x. 156.

would be obliged to judge as I do. If it were not so, we should never think of arguing. We should simply say, "Perhaps his mind is differently constituted from mine," as, in fact, with reference to special sets of dominant ideas, and to special provinces of experience, we often do say. But these we regard as hindrances, imperfections, accidents. We do not doubt that the system of reason is active in him as in us.

And thus, as reason is essentially a system, the universality of judgment involves something more. We not only think that our judgment is obligatory upon every one else, in as far as they have the same materials, but we think that it must be *consistent with* the judgments of all other persons, just as much as with our own. If it is inconsistent with any other judgment, we think that one of the two must be wrong ; that is, we will not admit the possibility that the real world, as others construct it, is out of harmony with the real world as we construct it.

Thus knowledge, being judgment, is necessary and universal, and in the widest sense this is true of all judgments.

(γ) These are two properties of the Judgment, but they do not tell us what it is. We shall of course examine its nature more fully in the later lectures. At present we need only think of it as affirmation. This may be simply described as "pronouncing the interpretation of our perceptions to form one system with the data of our perceptions." We may at once admit the distinction between *data* and interpretation to be only relative. Its relativity is the consequence of the constructed or so to speak artificial

Judgment is constructive.

character of our real world. We can get at no data un-
qualified by judgment.

We may take as an example our perception of things in
space. How much of what we see is given in present
sense-perception? This is a question to which there is no
definite answer. We do not know what the presentations
of vision were like before we had learnt to see as a fully
conscious human being sees. We have no right to assume,
that after we have learned to see in this way the actual
sense-presentation remains the same as it was in a different
stage of our visual education. We can give no precise
meaning in the way of a time-limit to the *presentness* of
perception. But we know this much, that it takes a long
time and many kinds of experience to learn to see as an
educated human being sees, and that this acquired capacity
is never at a stand-still, but is always being extended or
diminished according to the vitality, growth, or atrophy of
our apperceptive masses. There is always a certain element
of amplification or interpretation, which by experience or
attentive introspection we can eliminate from the data
apparently forced upon us by reality, although these
data themselves are modified through and through both
by habitual interpretation, and by the very defining attention which aims at eliminating all amplification from
them.

But yet the whole of sense-perception has a peculiar
quality in being *present*. Artificial though it is, it yet,
relatively speaking, contains an irreducible datum. It is
distinguishable from everything which is not present. It is
pervaded by something which we cannot reduce to intel-

lectual relation, though if we withdrew from it all that is relation, the apparent datum would be gone.

Now Knowledge is the affirmation or judgment which identifies the constructive interpretation of our present perception with the reality which present perception forces upon us. This is clear enough to begin with, but will have to be modified below to suit the more circuitous or mediate types of Judgment.

I take two examples, one from sight and one from sound.

Here is a table. In common language we should all say, "We see that is a table." The expression is quite correct, because human seeing is a judgment. But yet, if you were asked to reduce your perception to terms of sight pure and simple—I mean of visual sensation—why, unless you were an analytic psychologist or a very skilful artist, you would not be able to do it. To speak of one point only, you would have to eliminate the attribute of depth and distance. That is all, so far as mere vision is concerned, your theory and your interpretation. The problem for an artist is to get back, at his high plane of perceptive power, to what in theory would be the lower plane. He has to re-translate his perception of a thing in space into a flat coloured surface. The difference between his flat picture and a real object in space is a rough measure of the difference made by interpretation or implication in the datum of sense-perception when we say, judging by sight only, "That is a table." All the experiences of touch and motion, from which we have learned to perceive the solidity of the object, are, theoretically speaking, put into the judgment by us. They are not given by the eye alone, although we cannot now separate them from that which is given by the eye alone. For the artist's flat picture, which I used as an illustration, is not a stage in our visual education. Our visual education has proceeded *pari passu* with our education by touch and motion ; and we saw objects in space as solids, long before we reflected that for the eye alone a coloured surface would naturally appear as flat.[1]

But this impossibility of getting at an original datum only shows how entirely we are right in saying that our world is constructed by judgment. For the process of interpretative amplification passes quite continuously from the unconscious to the conscious ; and every definitely expressed judgment, though perfectly homogeneous with the processes which have qualified its datum, and though it may fall wholly within the maximum of what in ordinary parlance we should call a simple given perception, contains an identification of some ideal element, enlargement, or interpretation, with that relatively given element which reveals itself through a peculiar quality of presentness pervading the "given" perception.

In the example " That is a table," the unity of judgment is so well shown that the identification becomes almost unreal. In fact, we never judge except to satisfy an interest, and so simple a judgment used as an example, apart from any context which could explain the need for it, has an air of unreality. You may hear a child make such a judgment

[1] The view that depth is a visual datum in the same sense as breadth seems to me in flagrant contradiction with experience. But for our present purpose the question is only one of degree, as no one maintains that either depth or breadth are seen without education as an adult sees them.

constantly in the sheer pleasure of recognition. An adult would never make it explicitly unless in some particular context; but it is made, as I shall maintain below, by the mere glance of his eye which takes in the table as a real object in a real world of space. Its appearance to the eye is in this case the datum, while the interpretation consists in construing this appearance as a solid individual existence in space.

We will look at an example in which the discrimination of elements is easier. Take the affirmation, "That is a cab," assuming it to be made from merely hearing a sound. In this we can much more nearly separate the datum or minimum of sense from our enlargement or interpretation of it, and we know that our interpretation is liable to be wrong; that is to say, the reality into which we ought to construe the sound may be some other kind of vehicle, and not a cab. Now compare this with the affirmation, "That (which I see) is a cab." This judgment of sight-perception, though its terms are more inextricably interwoven, has just the same elements in it as the judgment of sound-perception, "That (which I hear) is a cab." In the sound-perception the structure is quite plain. A particular complex quality in the sound suggests as its objective explanation, what is perfectly distinguishable from it in thought, the movement of a cab on a particular kind of pavement. The quality of the sound, its roughness, loudness, increase and decrease, all form points of connection with the sound of a cab as we know it, and with the speed, weight, etc. of such a vehicle. But it is quite easy to consider the sound in itself apart from its interpretation, and we sometimes feel the interpretation to be more immediate, and sometimes more inferential. We sometimes say, "I hear a cab," just as we say, "I see one," but in case of sound we more often perhaps say, "That sounds like—" such and such a thing, which indicates a doubt, and the beginning of conscious inference.

Thus we see how continuous is the mental construction of reality. From our unreflective education in seeing, hearing, and touching, to the explicit judgment of the trained observer, which in its turn passes readily into inference, there is no definite break. Once the idea of reality, or of a world, is applied in practice (I do not say reflectively grasped), there is no further difficulty in principle throughout the whole process of its construction.

We may then sum up so far: our knowledge, or our world in knowledge, exists for us as a judgment, that is, as an affirmation in which our present perception is amplified by an ideal interpretation which is identified with it. This interpretation or enlargement claims necessity or universality, and is therefore objective as our world, *i. e.* is what we are *obliged* to think, and what we are *all* obliged to think. The whole system in process of construction, viz. our present perception as extended by interpretation, is what we mean by reality, only with a reservation in favour of forms of experience which are not intellectual at all. Every judgment then affirms something to be real, and therefore affirms reality to be defined, in part, by that something. Knowledge exists in the form of affirmations about reality. And our world as existing for us in the medium of knowledge consists, for us, of a standing affirmation about reality.

4. This standing affirmation about reality may be described in other words as " the continuous affirmative judgment of the waking consciousness." In the common logic-books you will find judgment treated only as the "proposition," that is, as an assertion made in language. That is a very convenient way of treating the judgment, and is not false, if you remember that the proposition, that is, the assertory sentence, is rather a translation of the judgment than the judgment itself. But the judgment expressed in a proposition is always some one definite assertion, with a limited subject and predicate. We shall speak of the judgment in this sense—the usual sense—later. But to-day I want to describe the judgment in a more extended sense, that is, as co-extensive with the waking human consciousness, so far as aware of a world.

If judgment consists in the extension of our perceptions by an interpretation considered as equally real with their content, it clearly is not confined to the particular facts and truths which from time to time we utter in language. And more than this, everything that we do definitely utter, im-plies a great deal which is not definitely uttered. If I say, " I have to catch the train at Sloane Square to go down to Essex Hall," I only mention the reality of one train, one square, and one building. But my assertion shades off into innumerable facts, the equal reality of which as elements in my world is necessary to make this judgment intelligible and true. It implies the real existence of the underground rail-way, which implies that of London, and therefore that of the surface of our globe in a certain definite order, and of the civilised world. It implies the reality of this building and of the meetings which we hold in it, of the University

Extension system, and of my own life and habits as enabling me to take part in the work of that system. Only a part of this is in the focus of my attention as I judge; but the whole is a continuous context, the parts of which are inseparable; and although I do not affirm the whole of it in so many words, when I say that I am coming down here by train this evening, yet if any part of it was not affirmed the rest would, so to speak, fall to pieces, *i. e.* would lose relations in the absence of which its meaning would be destroyed. Other detached parts of one's life and knowledge may seem to be separable from the content of such a judgment; but on looking closely we see that this is not the case. So long as we are awake, our whole world is conceived as real, and forms for us a single immense affirmation, which hangs from present perception, and shares its constraining power. My present perception is the illuminated spot, and shades off gradually into the rest which forms the background, receiving from this background its organised systematic individuality, while impressing upon it a relation to its own sensuous presentness. We have only to reflect, in order to illustrate this connection, on the way in which the idea of London forms a determining background for the present perception of this room, while on the other hand it is perceived by us as real in our presentation of this room.

And indeed the simplest example of what I am pointing out is the arrangement of objects and places in space. The visual picture which each of us forms of this room is certainly an affirmative judgment. It is a judgment because it consists of ideas affirmed as true of reality. As we look round, all the distances of the objects and the walls from

each other, and their shapes and position, seem to be im-
printed on our minds without an effort. But really they are
conclusions from long education in the art of seeing and
from the experience of the other senses. They are an enlargement or interpretation of sense-perception, taken as real,
i. e. as forming a system which is one with the content of
sense-perception, and touches us through sense-perception,
and therefore they exist for us in the form of Judgment.
And, as I described before, our whole world, both of things
in space and of our own history and circumstances, is also
affirmed as the background implied in this picture. That
is to say, it is all connected together, it is all taken as equally
real, and it is all vouched for by its connection with what is
given to us in perception. What do we mean by saying
that the Antipodes are real, and implied in my perception of
this room? We mean that they are an element, necessary
to educated thought, in the same system with which I am in
contact at this moment by sight, touch, and hearing, the
system of reality. And though I may not have explicitly
thought of them since entering the room till now, yet, if
they were no part of my affirmed system of ideas, my perception of anything in space would be quite different from
what it is.

This sense of necessary connection is confined, I think, to
our *waking* consciousness. Of course there are degrees
between waking and dreaming ; but I should be inclined to
set up the presence or absence of judgment as a very fair
test of those degrees. We say that a man is *awake* in as far
as he is aware (i.) of a reality which is not his mere course
of consciousness, and (ii.) of the same reality of which other

people are aware; *i. e.* in as far as he identifies his present perception with a reality, and that the real reality. It is said that surprise, *i. e.* the sense of conflict between expectation and the reality, is absent in dreams, and in a very remarkable passage Æschylus identifies the life of the savage in his (imaginary) primitive state with a dream-life, considered as a life of sensuous presentation, in which the interpretative judgment of perception was absent. With extraordinary profoundness, in portraying this all but animal existence, he strikes out all those relations to the objective world by which man forms for himself a system that goes beyond the present, so as to leave the stream of presentation without any background of organised reality.[1]

[1] I quote from Mrs. Browning's Translation of the *Prometheus Bound*, which seems close enough for the present purpose.

> " And let me tell you, not as taunting men,
>   But teaching you the intention of my gifts,
>   How first, *beholding, they beheld in vain,*
>   *And hearing, heard not,* but, *like shapes in dreams,*
>   Mixed all things wildly down the tedious time,
>   Nor knew to build a house against the sun
>   With wicketed sides, nor any woodwork knew,
>   But lived, like silly ants, beneath the ground,
>   In hollow caves unsunned.   There came to them
>   No steadfast sign of winter, nor of spring
>   Flower-perfumed, nor of summer full of fruit,
>   But blindly and lawlessly they did all things,
>   Until I taught them how the stars do rise
>   And set in mystery, and devised for them
>   Number, the inducer of philosophies,
>   The synthesis of letters, and besides,
>   The artificer of all things, Memory,
>   That sweet muse-mother."—*Pr.*, v. 445, ft.

The expression " seeing saw not, and hearing heard not " appears to suggest the contrast of presentation and objective perception.

It may be asked, " Why should not a man form for himself a system which interprets his own perception, but is discrepant from the system of every one else ? Should we in that case count him as awake ? " Yes, he would be awake, but he would be mad. Suppose, being a common man, he interprets all his perceptions into a system which makes him out to be King of England ; in such a case he cannot be set down as dreaming, because he is alleging a connection which goes beyond his present perception, and has, ostensibly, been propounded as an interpretation of it into a systematic order of things. He has in short *a* world, but he has broken away from *the* world, and therefore we pronounce him mad. A completely new vision of life may cause a man to be thought mad.[1]

The whole world, then, of our waking [2] consciousness may be treated as a single connected predicate affirmed as an enlargement of present perception. All that we take to be real is by the mere fact of being so taken, brought within an affirmative judgment.

5. To further illustrate the relation of what, in our permanent judgment, is distinctly thought, what is dimly thought, and what is implied, let us look for a moment at what we may call " the world as will." This is *not* the doctrine of Schopenhauer in his work, *The World as Will and Idea,*

Comparison with world as Will.

[1] See Browning's *Epistle of Karshish.*

[2] I do not mean to say that judgment and consciousness of a world can be wholly absent in dreams, and often no doubt they are distinctly present. But in those dreams, in my own experience the normal ones, which leave behind a mere impression that unrecognisable images have passed before the mind, judgment and the sense of reality must surely have all but disappeared. I am inclined to think that dreams are very much rationalised in recollection and description.

although the two conceptions have something in common. His is a metaphysical doctrine, in which he says that the fundamental reality of the Universe must be conceived as Will. We have nothing to do with that. We are speaking merely of what the world is for us, and for us it is not only a system of reality but a system of purposes. Our world of will is a permanent factor of our waking consciousness, just as much as our world of knowledge. Now our will is made up of a great number of purposes, more or less connected together, just as our knowledge is made up of a great number of provinces and regions more or less connected together. And just as in our knowledge at any moment much is clear, much is dim, much is implied, and the whole forms a continuous context, so it is with our purposes

When, for example, one stands looking at a picture, one's immediate conscious purpose is to study the picture. One also entertains dimly or by force of habit the purpose to remain standing, which is a curious though common instance of will. We do not attend to the purpose of walking or standing, yet we only walk or stand (in normal conditions of mind) as long as we will to do so. If we go to sleep or faint, we shall fall down. Purpose, like judgment, is confined to the waking consciousness.

But further; the purpose which one entertains in standing to look at a picture is not really an isolated pin-point of will. It is uppermost in the mind at the moment in which we carry it out, but it is only the uppermost stratum, or perhaps rather the present point attained upon a definite road, within an intricate formation or network of purposes, which taken together constitute the world of will. The purpose of looking at a picture shades off into the more general purpose of learning to take pleasure in what is good of its kind, which is again set in a certain place within the conception of our life and the way in which we desire to spend it, and our purposes throughout every particular day are fitted into one another, and give a particular setting and colour to each other, and to each particular day, and week, and year.

Now less or more of all this may be clearly in the mind when we are carrying out a particular momentary aim. But it is quite certain that in a human life the particular momentary aim derives its significance from this background of other purposes ; and, if they were to fall away, the distinct momentary purpose would change its character and become quite a feeble and empty thing.

Thus we have, in our world of will, a parallel case which illustrates the nature of our world of knowledge. There is the clear will to look at the picture, the dim will to continue standing, and the implied will to carry out certain general aims, and follow a certain routine or course of life, which gives the momentary purpose its entire setting and background.

I have spoken of the will in order to illustrate the judgment, because the dim and implied elements are perhaps more easy to observe in the case of the will. Almost all our common waking life is carried on by actions such as walking and sitting, which we hardly know that we will, but which we could not do if we did not will them. And also the greater part of our life is rather within a sphere of will which has become objective for us in our profession, interests, and ideals, than a perpetual active choice between alternatives such as brings the act of volition before us in the most striking way. Just so it is with judgment. Our speaking and writing is a very small part of our judging, just as our conscious choice between alternatives[1] is a very small part of our willing.

Distribution of Attention.

6. Thus the world of knowledge and the world of will must each of them be regarded as a *continuum* for the waking consciousness. Whenever we are awake, we are judging ; whenever we are awake we are willing. The distribution of attention in these two worlds is very closely analogous. In both, it is impossible to attend to our whole world at the same moment. But in both, our world is taken as being a single connected system ; and therefore (i.) attention shades off gradually from the momentary focus of illumination into less and less intensity over the other parts of the continuous judgment or purpose ; but (ii.) that which is *in* the focus of attention depends for its quality upon that which is less distinctly or not at all in the focus of attention. And as attention diminishes in intensity, the implication of reality does not diminish with it. In other words, in spite of the inequality of attention, the reality of our whole world is implied in the reality of which at any moment we are distinctly aware. But being distinctly aware of reality is another name for judgment.

Now the common logical judgments which we shall have to analyse and classify are simply those parts of this continuous affirmation of consciousness which are from time

[1] I do not for a moment suggest that our "conscious choice" is ultimately different in kind from our habitual persistence in a course of life. I only take it as an instance in which we fully attend to our volition.

to time separately made distinct.   Each of them therefore
must be regarded as a partial expression of the nature of
reality, and the subject will always be Reality in one form,
and the predicate reality in another form.   The ultimate
and complete judgment would be the whole of Reality
predicated of itself.   All our logical judgments are such
portions and fragments of this judgment as we can grasp
at the moment.   Some of these gather up in a system
whole provinces of reality, others merely enlarge, interpret,
or analyse the content of a very simple sense-perception.
We shall not go far wrong in practice if we start from this
judgment of Perception as the fundamental kind of Judgment.   The real subject in Judgment is always Reality in
some particular datum or qualification, and the tendency
of Judgment is always to be a definition of Reality.   We
see the parts of Judgment most clearly in such thoughts as
"This is blue"; "This is a flower"; "That light is the
rising sun"; "That sound is the surf on a sandy shore."
In these we can plainly distinguish the element of presentation and the interpretative construction or analytic synthesis
which is by the judgment identified with it.

LECTURE III

THE RELATION OF LOGIC TO KNOWLEDGE

Meaning of "Form." 1. I SPOKE of the whole world, which we take to be real, as presented to us in the shape of a continuous judgment. It is the task of Logic to analyse the structure of this Judgment, the parts of which are Judgments.

The first thing is then to consider what sort of properties of Judgments we attend to in Logic. It is commonly said that Logic is a formal science ; that is, that it deals with the form, and not with the content or matter of knowledge.

This word "form" is always meeting us in philosophy. "Species" is Latin for form, as εἶδος and ἰδέα are Greek for form. The form of any object primarily means its appearance, that which the mind can carry away, while the object as a physical reality, as material, remains where it was. It need not mean shape as opposed to colour ; that is a narrower usage. The Greek opinion was no doubt rooted in some such notion as that in knowing or remembering a thing the mind possessed its form or image without its matter. Thus the form came to stand for the knowable shape or structure which makes a thing what it is, and by which we recognise it when we see it. This was its species or its idea, the "image," as it is used in the phrase, "Let us make man in our own image." So in any work of the hands of man, the form was the shape given by the workman, and came out of his mind, while the matter was the stuff or material out of which the thing was made.

The moment we contemplate a classification of the sciences, we see that this is a purely relative distinction. There is no matter without form. If it was in this deep sense without form, it would be without properties, and so incapable of acting or being acted upon. In a knife the matter is steel, the form is the shape of the blade. But the qualities of steel again depend, we must suppose, upon a certain character and arrangement in its particles, and this is, as Bacon would have called it, the *form* of steel. But taken as purely relative, the distinction is good *prima facie*. Steel has its own form, but the knife has its form, and the matter steel can take many other forms besides that of a knife. Marble has its own form, its definable properties as marble (chemical and mechanical), but in a statue, marble is the matter, and the form is the shape given by the sculptor.

Now applying this distinction to knowledge in general, we see that all science is formal, and therefore it is no distinction to say that Logic is a formal science. Geometry is a formal science ; even molecular physics is a formal science. All science is formal, because all science consists in tracing out the universal characteristics of things, the structure that makes them what they are.

The particular "form," then, with which a science deals is simply the kind of properties that come under the point of view from which that science in particular looks at things. But a very general science is more emphatically formal than a very special science. That is to say, it deals with properties which are presented in some degree by everything ; and so in every object a great multitude of properties are disregarded by it, are treated by it as matter and not as form. In this sense Logic is emphatically "formal," though not nearly so formal as it is often supposed to be. The subject-matter of Logic, then, is Knowledge *qua* Knowledge, or the form of knowledge ; that is, the properties which are possessed by objects or ideas *in so far as they are members of the world of knowledge*. And it is quite essential to distinguish the form of knowledge in this sense from its matter or content. The "matter" of knowledge is the whole region of facts dealt with by science and perception. If Logic dealt with this in the way in which knowledge deals with it, *i. e* simply as a process of acquiring and organising experience, then Logic would simply be another name for the whole range of science, history, and perception. Then there would be no distinction between logic and science or common sense, and in trying to ascertain, say, the wave-length of red light, or the cab-fare from Chelsea to Essex Hall, we should be investigating a logical problem. But we see at once that this is not what we mean by studying knowledge as knowledge. Science or common sense aims at a particular answer to each problem of this kind. Logic aims at understanding the type and principles both of the problem and of its answer. The details of the particular answer are the "*matter* of fact." The type and principles which are found in all such particular answers may be regarded as the form of fact, *i. e.* that which makes the fact a fact in knowledge.

Jevons appears to me to make a terrible blunder at this

point. He says[1]—"One name which has been given to Logic, namely the Science of Sciences, very aptly describes the all-extensive power of logical principles. The cultivators of special branches of knowledge appear to have been fully aware of the allegiance they owe to the highest of the sciences, for they have usually given names implying this allegiance. The very name of Logic occurs as part of nearly all the names adopted for the sciences, which are often vulgarly called the 'ologies,' but are really the 'logics,' the 'o' being only a connecting vowel or part of the previous word. Thus geology is logic applied to explain the formation of the earth's crust; biology is logic applied to the phenomena of life ; psychology is logic applied to the nature of the mind ; and the same is the case with physiology, entomology, zoology, teratology, morphology, anthropology, theology, ecclesiology, thalattology, and the rest. Each science is thus distinctly confessed to be a special logic. The name of Logic itself is derived from the common Greek word λόγος, which usually means *word*, or the sign and outward manifestation of any inward thought. But the same word was also used to denote the inward thought or reasoning of which words are the expression, and it is thus probably that later Greek writers on reasoning were led to call their science ἐπιστήμη λογικἡ, or logical science, also τέχνη λογικἡ, or logical art. The adjective λογικἡ, being used alone, soon came to be the name of the science, just as Mathematic, Rhetoric, and other names ending in 'ic' were originally adjectives, but have been converted into substantives."

[1] *Elementary Lessons,* p. 6.

This account of the connection between the name
"Logic" and the terminations of the names of the sciences
appears precisely wrong. Whatever may have been the
exact meaning of the expression "Logic," or "Logical
curriculum,"[1] or "art," or "science" when first employed,
there can be no doubt that the word logical had a substantive reference to that about which the science or teaching
in question was to treat. The term "logic," therefore,
corresponds not to the syllables "logy" in such a word as
"Zoology," but to the syllables "Zoo," which indicate the
province of the special science, and not its character as a
science. Zoology means connected discourse (λόγος) about
living creatures. Logic meant a curriculum, or science or
art dealing with connected discourse. The phrase "Science
of Sciences," rightly interpreted, has the same meaning. It
does not mean that Logic is a Science which comprises all
the special sciences, but that Logic is a Science dealing with
those general properties and relations which all sciences *qua*
sciences have in common, but omitting, as from its point of
view matter and not form, the particular details of content
by which every science answers the particular questions
which it asks. It is wild, and most mischievous, to say that
"every science is a special logic," or that "biology is Logic
applied to the phenomena of life." This confusion destroys
the whole disinterestedness which is necessary to true scientific Logic, and causes the logical student always to have
his eye on puzzles, and special methods, and interferences
by which he may teach the student of science how to perform the concrete labour of research. We quite admit that

---

[1] πραγμάτεια. See Prantl, i. 545.

a looker-on may *sometimes* see more of the game, and no wise investigator would contemn *a priori* the suggestions of a student like Goethe, or Mill, or Lotze, because their author was not exclusively engaged in the observation of nature. But all this is secondary. The idea that Logic is a judge of scientific results, able to pass sentence, in virtue of some general criterion, upon their validity and invalidity, arises from a deep-lying misconception of the nature of truth which naturally allies itself with the above confusion between Logic and the special sciences.

Therefore the relation between content or matter of knowledge, and the form which is its general characteristic as knowledge, is of this kind. We can either study the objects of knowledge directly as we perceive them, or indirectly, as examples of the way in which we know. As studied for their own sake, they are regarded as the matter or content in which the general form of knowledge finds individual realisation. In botany, for instance, we have a large number of actual plants classified and explained in their relation to one another. A botanist is interested directly in the affinities and evolution of these plants, and in the principles of biology which underlie their history. He pushes his researches further and further into the individual matters that come to light, without, as a rule, more than a passing reflection upon the abstract nature of the methods which he is creating as his work proceeds. He classifies, explains, observes, experiments, theorises, generalises, to the best of his power, solely in order to grasp and render intelligible the region of concrete fact that lies before him. Now while his particular results and discoveries constitute the "form" or knowable properties of the plant-world *as the object of botanical science*, the science which inquires into the general nature of knowledge must treat these particular results as "mere matter"—as something with which it is not directly concerned, any more than the art which makes a statue is primarily and directly concerned with the chemical and mechanical properties of marble. The "form" or knowable properties with which the general science of knowledge is directly concerned, consists in those methods and processes which the man of science, developing the modes in which common sense naturally works, constructs unconsciously as he goes along. Thus, not the nature and affinities of the plant-world, but classification, explanation, observation, experiment, theory, are the phenomena in virtue of which the organised structure of botanical science participates in the form of knowledge, and its objects become, in these respects, objects of logical theory.

Hence some properties and relations of objects, being the form or knowable structure of the concrete objects as a special department of nature, correspond to the mere matter, stuff, or content of Knowledge in general, while other properties and relations of objects, being their form or knowable structure as entering into a world of reality displayed to our intelligence, correspond to the form of Knowledge as treated of by a general inquiry into its characteristics, which we call Logic. It is just as the qualities or "forms" of the different metals of which knives can be made are mere matter or irrelevant detail when we are discussing the general "form" or quality of a good knife,

whatever its material.   A reservation on this head appears
in the following section.

2. For the form of Knowledge depends in some de- Form of
gree upon its matter.   It is very important to realise this Know-ledge de-
truth ; for if Logic is swamped by being identified with the pendent on Content.
whole range of special sciences, it is killed by being emptied
of all adaptation to living intelligence.   What is called
Formal Logic *par excellence*, in all its shapes, whether anti-
quated as in Hamilton's or Thomson's Formal Laws of
Thought, or freshly worked out on a symbolic basis as by
Boole and others, has, it appears to me, this initial defect,
when considered as a general theory of Logic.   As a contribu-
tion to such a theory, every method which will work undoubtedly has its place, and indicates and depends upon
some characteristic of real thought.   But in the central
theory itself, and especially in so short an account of it as
must be attempted in these lectures, I should be inclined to
condemn all attempts to employ symbols for anything more
than the most passing illustration of points in logical processes.   All such attempts, I must maintain, share with the
old-fashioned laws of Identity, Contradiction, and Excluded
Middle the initial fallacy of representing a judgment by
something which is not and cannot be in any way an
adequate symbol of one.   If, in order to get at the pure
form of Knowledge, we restrict ourselves to very abstract
characteristics in which all knowledge appears, very roughly
speaking, to agree, and which can be symbolized for working
purposes by combinations of signs which have not the
essential properties of ideal contents, then we have *ab initio*
substituted for the judgment something which is a very

abstract corollary from the nature of judgment, and may or not for certain purposes and within certain limits be a fair representative of it. We cannot and must not exclude from the form of Knowledge its modifications according to "matter," and its nature as existing only in "matter."

In fact, the peculiar "form" of *everything* depends in some degree on its "matter." A statue in marble is a little differently treated if it is copied in bronze. A knife is properly made of steel; you can only make a bad one of iron, or copper, or flint, and you cannot make one at all of wax. Different matters will more or less take the same form, but only within certain limits. So it is in Knowledge. The *nature of objects as Knowledge*—for we *must* remember that "form" in our sense is not something put into the "matter," something alien or indifferent to it, but is simply its own inmost character revealed by the structural relations in which it is found capable of standing [1]—depends on the way in which their parts are connected together.

Let us compare, for example, the use of number in understanding objects of different kinds.

Suppose there are four books in a heap on the table. This heap of books is the object. We desire to conceive it as a whole consisting of parts. In order to do so we simply *count* them "one, two, three, *four* books." If one is taken away, there is one less to count; if one is added, there is one more. But the books themselves, as books, are not

---

[1] The example of the marble statue may seem to contradict this idea; and no doubt the indifference of matter to form is a question of degree. But the feeling for material is a most important element in fine art; and in knowledge there is only a relative distinction between formal and material relations.

altered by taking away one from them or adding one to them. They are parts indifferent to each other, forming a heap which is sufficiently analysed or synthesised by counting its parts.

But now instead of four books in a heap, let us think of the four sides of a square. Of course we *can* count them, as we counted the books; but we have not conceived the nature of the square by counting its sides. That does not distinguish it from four straight lines drawn anyhow in space. In order to appreciate what a square is, we must consider that the sides are *equal* straight lines, put together in a particular way so as to make a figure with four right angles; we must distinguish it from a figure with four equal sides, but its angles not right angles, and from a four-sided figure with right angles, but with only its opposite sides equal; and note that if we shorten up one side into nothing, the square becomes a triangle, with altogether different properties from those of a square; if we put in another side it becomes a pentagon, and so on.

These two things, the heap of books and the square, are *prima facie* objects of perception. We commonly speak of a diagram on a blackboard or in a book as "a square" if we have reason to take it as approximately exact, and as intended for a square. But on looking closer, we soon see that the "matter," or individual attributes, of each of these objects of our apprehension demands a different form of knowledge from that necessary to the other. The judgment " *This* heap of books has four books in it" is a judgment of enumerative perception. The judgment " *The* square has four sides" is a judgment of systematic necessity.

Why did we not keep the two judgments in the same logical shape? Why did we say "*This* heap" and "*The* square"? Why did we not say "this" in both propositions, or "the" in both propositions? Because the different "matter" demands this difference of form. Let us try. "The heap of books has four books in it." Probably we interpret this proposition to mean just the same as if we had said "This heap." That is owing to the fact that the judgment naturally occurs to us in its right form. But if we interpret "The heap" on the analogy of our interpretation of "The square," our judgment will have become false.

It will have come to mean "Every heap of books has four books in it," and a judgment of perception will not bear this enlargement. The subject is composite, and one, the most essential of its elements, is destroyed by the change from "this" to "the."

Let us try again. Let us say "This square has four sides." That is not exactly false, but it is ridiculous. Every square must have four sides, and by saying "this square" we strongly imply that foursidedness is a relation of which we are aware chiefly, if not exclusively, in the object attended to in the moment of judging, simply through the apprehension of that moment. By this implication the form of the judgment abandons and all but denies the character of systematic necessity which its content naturally demands. It is like saying, "It appears to me that in the present instance two and two make four." The number of sides in a square, then, is not a mere fact of perception, while the number of books in a heap is in such a fact.

But you may answer by suggesting the case that an uninstructed person—say a child, with a square figure before him, and having heard the name square applied to figures generally resembling that figure, may simply observe the number of sides, without knowing any of the geometrical properties connected with it; will he not then be right in saying, "This square has four sides"?

Certainly not. In that case he has no right to call it a square. It would only be a name he had picked up without knowing what it meant. All he has the right to say would be, "This object" or "This figure has four sides." That would be a consistent judgment of mere perception, true as far as it went. It is always possible to apprehend the more complex objects of knowledge in the simpler forms; but then they are not apprehended adequately, not *as* complex objects. It is also possible to apply very complex forms of knowledge to very simple objects. Most truths that can be laid down quite in the abstract about a human mind could also be applied in some sense or other to any speck of protoplasm, or to any pebble on the seashore. And every simple form of knowledge is always being pushed on, by its own defects and inconsistencies, in the direction of more complex forms.

So far I have been trying to show that objects are capable of being different in their nature as knowledge as well as in their individual properties; and that their different natures as knowledge depend on the way in which their parts are connected together. We took two objects of knowledge, and found that the mode of connection between the parts required two quite different kinds of judgment to express them. Let us look at the reason of this.

The relation of Part and Whole.

3. The relation of Part and Whole is a form of the relation of Identity and Difference. Every Judgment expresses the unity of some parts in a whole, or of some differences in an Identity. This is the meaning of "construction" in knowledge. We saw that knowledge exists in judgment as a construction (taking this to include maintenance) of reality.

The expression whole and parts may be used in a strict or in a lax sense.

In a strict sense it means a whole of quantity, that is, a whole considered as made up by the addition of parts of the same kind, as a foot is made up of twelve inches. In this sense the whole is the sum of the parts. And even in this sense the whole is represented within every part by an identity of quality that runs through them all. Otherwise there would be nothing to earmark them as belonging to the particular whole or kind of whole in question. Parts of length make up a whole of length, parts of weight a whole of weight, parts of intensity a whole of intensity, in so far as a whole of intensity is quantitative, which is not a perfectly easy question. Wholes like these are "*Sums*" or "*Totals*." The relation of whole to part in this sense is a very simple case of the relation of differences in an identity, but for that very reason is not the easiest case to appreciate. The relation is so simple that it is apt to pass unnoticed, and in dealing with numerical computation we are apt to forget that in application to any concrete problem the numbers must be numbers of something having a common quality, and that the nature of this something may affect the result as related to real fact, though not as a conclusion from pure

numerical premisses. In a whole of pure number the indifference of parts to whole reaches its maximum. The unit
remains absolutely the same, into whatever total of addition
it may enter.

In a whole of differentiated members, such as a square,
all this begins to be different. A side in a square possesses,
by the fact of being a side, very different relations and
properties from those of a straight line conceived in isolation.
In this case the whole is not made up merely by adding
the parts together. It is a geometrical whole, and its parts
are combined according to a special form of necessity
which is rooted in the nature of space. Speaking generally, the point is that parts must occupy certain perfectly
definite places as regards each other. You cannot make
a square by merely adding three right angles to one, nor
by taking a given straight line and adding three more
equal straight lines to its length. You must construct
in a definite way so as to fulfil definite conditions. The
identity shows itself in the different elements which make it
up, not as a mere repeated quality, but as a property of
contributing, each part in a distinctive way, to the nature of
the whole. Such an identity is not a mere total or sum,
though I imagine that its relations can be fully expressed in
terms of quantity, certain differentiated objects or conceptions being given (*e. g.* line and angle).

I take a further instance to put a sharp point upon this
distinction. The relation of whole and parts is nowhere
more perfect, short of a living mind, than in a work of art.
There is a very fine Turner landscape now[1] in the " Old

[1] February 1892.

Masters" Exhibition at Burlington House—the picture of
the two bridges at Walton-on-Thames. The picture is full
of detail—figures, animals, trees, and a curving river-bed.
But I am told that if one attempts to cut out the smallest
appreciable fragment of all this detail, one will find that it
cannot be done without ruining the whole effect of the
picture. That means that the individual totality is so
welded together by the master's selective composition, that,
according to Aristotle's definition of a true "whole," if any
part is modified or removed the total is entirely altered,
"for that of which the presence or absence makes no
difference is no true part of the whole." [1]

Of course, in saying that the part is thus essential to the
whole, it is implied that the whole reacts upon and trans-
figures the part. It is in and by this transformation that its
pervading identity makes itself felt throughout all the
elements by which it is constituted. As the picture would
be ruined if a little patch of colour were removed, so the
little patch of colour might be such as to be devoid of all
value if seen on a piece of paper by itself. I will give an
extreme instance, almost amounting to a *tour de force*, from
the art of poetry, in illustration of this principle. We
constantly hear and use in daily life the phrase, "It all
comes to the same thing in the end." Perhaps in the very
commonest speech we use it less fully, omitting the word
"thing"; but the sentence as written above is a perfectly
familiar platitude, with no special import, nor grace of sound
or rhythm. Now, in one of the closing stanzas of Browning's
poem *Any Wife to Any Husband*, this sentence, only modified

[1] *Poetics*, 8.

by the substitution of "at" for "in," forms an entire line.[1] And I think it will generally be felt that there are few more stately and pathetic passages than this in modern poetry. Both the rhythm and sonorousness of the whole poem, and also its burden of ideal feeling, are communicated to the line in question by the context in which it is framed. Through the rhythm thus prescribed to it, and through the characteristic emotion which it contributes to reveal, the "whole" of the poem re-acts upon this part, and confers upon it a quality which, apart from such a setting, we should never have dreamed that it was capable of possessing.

We are not here concerned with the peculiar "æsthetic" nature of works of art, which makes them, although rational, nevertheless unique individuals. I only adduced the above examples to show, in unmistakable cases, what is actually meant when we speak of "a whole" as constituted by a pervading identity which exhibits itself in the congruous or co-operating nature of all the constituent parts. In wholes of a higher kind than the whole of mere quantity the parts no longer repeat each other. They are not merely distinct,

---

[1] In order to remind the reader of the effect of this passage it is necessary to quote a few lines before and after—

> " Re-issue words and looks from the old mint,
>   Pass them afresh, no matter whose the print,
>   Image and superscription once they bore !
>   Re-coin thyself and give it them to spend,—
>   It all comes to the same thing at the end,
>   Since mine thou wast, mine art and mine shalt be,
>   Faithful or faithless, sealing up the sum
>   Or lavish of my treasure, thou must come
>   Back to the heart's place here I keep for thee ! "

but different. Yet the common or continuous nature shows itself within each of them.

The parts of a sum-total, taking them for convenience of summation as equal parts, may be called units;[1] the parts of an abstract system, such as a geometrical figure, may be called elements (I cannot answer for mathematical usage), and the parts of a concrete system, an æsthetic product, a mind, or a society, might be called members.

But every kind of whole is an identity, and its parts are always differences within it.

Nature of Knowledge.

4. It will be well to sum up here what we have learnt of the nature of knowledge in general, before passing to the definition and classification of Judgment.

Knowledge is always Judgment. Judgment is constructive, for us, of the real world. Constructing the real world means interpreting or amplifying our present perception by what we are obliged to think, which we take as all belonging to a single system one with itself, and with what constrains us in sense-perception, and objective in the sense that its parts act on each other independently of our individual apprehension, and that we are obliged to think them thus. The process of construction is always that of exhibiting a whole in its parts, *i.e.* an identity in its differences ; that is to say, it is always both analytic and synthetic. The objects of knowledge differ in the mode of relation between their

---

[1] A unit of measurement implies in addition that it has been equated with some accepted standard. If I divide the length of my room into thirty equal parts, each part is a "unit" in the sum-total; but I have not measured the room till I have equated one such part with a known standard, and thus made it into a unit in the general system of length equations.

parts and the whole, and thus give rise to different types of judgment and inference; and this difference in the form of knowledge is a difference in the content of Logic, which deals with the objects of experience only from the point of view of their properties as objects in an intellectual world.

5. I hope that these general lectures, which, as I am quite Conclu-sion. aware, have anticipated the treatment of many difficult questions which they have not attempted to solve, have been successful in putting the problem of Logic before us with some degree of vividness. If this problem were thoroughly impressed upon our minds, I should say that we had already gained something definite from this course of study. The points which I desire to emphasise are two.

(1) I hope that we have learned to realise the world of our knowledge as a living growth, sustained by the energy of our intelligence; and to understand that we do not start with a ready-made world in common, but can only enter upon the inheritance of science and civilisation as the result of courage, labour, and reasonable perseverance; and further, that we retain this inheritance just as long as our endurance and capacity hold out, and no longer.

And (2) I have attempted to make clear that this living growth, our knowledge, is like the vegetable or animal world in being composed of infinite minor systems, each and all of which are at bottom the same function with corresponding parts or elements, modified by adaption to the environment. So that the task of analysing the form of judgment bears a certain resemblance to that of analysing the forms of plants. Just as from the single cell of the undifferentiated Alga, to the most highly organised flower or tree, we have the same formation, with its characteristic functions and operations, so from the undifferentiated judgment, which in linguistic form resembles an ejaculation or interjection, to the reasonable systems of exact or philosophical science, we find the same systematic function with corresponding elements.

But the world of knowledge has a unity which the world of organic individuals cannot claim ; and this whole system of functions is itself, for our intelligence, approximately a single function or system, corresponding in structure to each of its individual parts, as though the plant world or animal world were itself in turn a plant or animal. We cannot hope to exhaust the shapes taken by the pervading fundamental function of intelligence. We shall only attempt to understand the analogies and differences between some few of its leading types.

LECTURE IV

TYPES OF JUDGMENT AND THE GENERAL CONDITIONS INVOLVED IN ASSERTION

1. The question of correspondence between the types of Judgment and the orders of Knowledge was really antici- pated in discussing the relation between the content and the form of knowledge. We saw that the content or matter known determines on the whole the form or method of knowledge by which it can be known.

Correspondence between types of Judgment and nature of objects as Knowledge.

I give a few cases of this correspondence, not professing to complete the list. We should accustom ourselves to think of these forms as constituting a progression in the sense that each of them betrays a reference to an ideal of knowledge which in itself it is unable to fulfil, and therefore inevitably suggests some further or divergent form. And the defect by which the forms contradict the ideal, is felt by us as a defect in their grasp of reality, in their presentation of real connections.

a. We think of the judgment as predicating an ideal content of a subject indicated in present perception. But there are judgments which scarcely have an immediate subject at all, such as "How hot!" "Bad!" "It hurts!" In the judgments thus represented the true subject is some

"Impersonal" Judgment.

undefined aspect of the given complex presentation. Of course the words which we use are not an absolutely safe guide to the judgment—they may be merely an abbreviation. But there are typical judgments of this kind in which we merely mean to connect some namable content with that which can only be defined as the focus of attention at the moment. Such judgments might be called predications of mere quality. The only link by which they bind their parts into a whole is a feeling referred to our momentary surroundings. A *mere* quality, if not defined or analysed, or a feeling of pleasure or pain, is the sort of object which can be expressed in such a judgment.

Perceptive Judgment.
b. Then we have the very wide sphere of perceptive judgment, which we may most conveniently confine to judgments which have in the subject elements analogous to "This," "Here," "Now." Such particles as these indicate an effort to distinguish elements within the complex presented. They have no content beyond the reference to presentation, and, in "here" and "now," an implication that the present is taken in a particular kind of *continuum*. Otherwise they mean nothing more or other than is meant by pointing with the finger. We may or may not help out a "subject" of this kind by definite ideas attached to it as conditions of the judgment. If we do, we are already on the road to a new form of knowledge, incompatible with the judgment of perception. For so long as we keep a demonstrative, spatial or temporal, reference in the thought, the subject of judgment is not cut loose from our personal focus of presentation. And as the existence of such a focus is undeniable, we are secure against criticism so far as the

content of the subject is concerned. But if we begin to specify it, we do so at our peril.

Such judgments as these have been called "Analytic judgments of sense."[1] The term is not generally accepted in this meaning, but is conveniently illustrative of the nature of these judgments. It is intended to imply that they are a breaking up and reconstruction of what, in our usual loose way of talking, is said to be given in sense-perception. They remain on the whole within the complex of "that which" is presented.

From the point of view which we have taken, such judgments are not confined to what we think it worth while to *say*, but are the essence of every orderly and objective perception of the world around us. In a waking human consciousness nothing is unaffirmed.

We have no other term than perception to express the process which is employed in scientific observation and experiment. But it is plain that so soon as the judgment that refers to "This" is modified through the inevitable demand for qualification by exact ideas—"*This* hurts me," "*What* hurts you?" "This old sprain, at the pace we are walking"—a conflict of elements has arisen within the judgment. And as commonplace perception passes into scientific observation, the qualifying ideas, on which truth and relevancy depend, dwarf the importance of the "this," and ultimately oust it altogether. That is a simple case in which the ideal of knowledge and the nature of reality operate within the judgment to split asunder its primitive form. The subject as expressed by a pure demonstrative refuses to

[1] Mr. F. H. Bradley, *Principle of Logic*, p. 48.

take account either of truth, *i. e.* consistency with knowledge as a whole, or of relevancy, *i. e.* consistency with the relation involved in the particular predication that may be in question. Our commonplace perception halts between these two extremes.   It deals with the world of individual objects and persons, which, being already systematised according to our current observations and interests, has, so long as we keep to its order, a sufficient degree of truth and relevancy for the needs of daily life.   Thus if I say, "This book will do as a desk to write upon," the truth of the qualification "book" (*i. e.* the reality of the subject) is assumed on the ground of the facility of recognising a well-known "thing," while the relevancy of the qualification "book" is not questioned, because we accept an individual thing as an object of habitual interest *qua* individual, and do not demand that whenever it is named those properties alone should be indicated which are relevant to the purpose for which it is named.   The "thing" is a current coin of popular thought, and makes common perception workable without straining after a special relevancy in the subject of every predication.   Such special relevancy leads ultimately to the ideal of *definition*, in which subject and predicate are adequate to each other and necessarily connected.   A definitory judgment drops the demonstrative and relies on qualifying ideas alone.   It is therefore an abstract universal Judgment, while the Judgment of Perception, so long as it retains the demonstrative, is a Singular Judgment.

Proper names in Judgment.

c. But a very curious example of a divergence or half-way house in Knowledge is that form of the singular Judgment in which the subject is a proper name.   A proper name is designative and not definitory. It may be described as a generalised demonstrative pronoun—a demonstrative pronoun which has the same particular reference in the mouth of every one who uses it, and beyond the given present of time.

So the reference of a proper name is a good example of what we called a universal or an identity. That which is referred to by such a name is a person or thing whose existence is extended in time and its parts bound together by some continuous quality—an *individual* person or thing and the whole of this individuality is referred to in whatever is affirmed about it. Thus the reference of such a name is universal, not as including more than one individual, but as including in the identity of the individual numberless differences—the acts, events, and relations that make up its history and situation.

What kinds of things are called by Proper Names, and why? This question is akin to the doctrine of Connotation and Denotation, which will be discussed in the next lecture. It is a very good problem to think over beforehand, noting especially the limiting cases, in which either some *people* give proper names to things to which other people do not give them, or some *things* are given proper names while other things of the same general kind are not. These judgments, which are both Singular and Universal, may perhaps be called for distinction's sake " Individual " Judgments.

d. The demonstrative perception may also be replaced by Abstract a more or less complete analysis or definition. Judgment

Within this province Definition of a concrete whole is one extreme, *e. g.* " Human Society is a system of wills " ;

F

that of an abstract whole the other extreme, " $12 = 7 + 5$."
There are all degrees, between these two, in the amount of
modification which the parts undergo by belonging to the
whole.   There are also all sorts of incomplete definitions,
expressing merely the effects of single conditions out of
those which go to make up a whole.   These form the
abstract universal judgments of the exact sciences, such as,
" If water is heated to 212° Fahr. under one atmosphere it
boils."   In all these cases some idea, " abstract " as being
cut loose from the focus of present perception, whether
abstract or concrete in its content, replaces the demonstrative
of the judgment which is a perception.   These are the
judgments which in the ordinary logical classification rank
as universal.

The gene-
ral defini-
tion of
Judgment.

2. It was quite right of us to consider some types of judgment before trying to define it generally.   It is hopeless to
understand a definition unless the object to be defined is
tolerably familiar.   We have said a great deal about knowledge and about judgment as the organ or medium of knowledge.   Now we want to study particular judgments in their
parts and working, and observe how they perform their
function of constructing reality.

Now, for our purpose, we may take the clearest cases of
judgment, viz. the meanings of propositions.

The distinctive character of Judgment as contrasted with
every other act of mind is that it claims to be true, *i. e.*
pre-supposes the distinction between truth and falsity.

First, we have to consider what is implied in claiming
truth.

Secondly, by what means truth is claimed in Judgment.

Thirdly, the nature of the ideas for which alone truth can be claimed.

(i.) Claiming truth implies the distinction between truth and falsity. I do not say, "between truth and falsehood," because falsehood includes a lie, and a lie is not, *prima facie*, an error or falsity of knowledge. It is, as may be said of a question, altogether addressed to another person, and has no existence as a distinct species within knowledge. Thus a lie is called by Plato "falsehood in words"; the term "falsehood in the mind" he reserves for ignorance or error, which he treats as the worst of the two, which from an intellectual point of view it plainly is.

What is implied in claiming truth.

No distinction between truth and falsity can exist unless, in the act or state which claims truth, there is a reference to something outside psychical occurrence in the course of ideas. Falsity or error are relations that imply existences which, having reality of one kind, claim in addition to this another kind of reality which they have not. In fact, all things that are called false, are called so because they claim a place or property which they do not possess. They must exist, in order to be false. It is in the non-fulfilment, by their existence, of some claim or pretension which it suggests, that falsity consists. And so it is in the fulfilment of such a claim that truth has a meaning. A false coin exists as a piece of metal ; it is false because it pretends to a place in the monetary system which its properties or history[1] contradict.

As the claim to be true is made by every judgment in its

[1] For it is, I suppose, technically false, even if over value, if not coined by those who have the exclusive legal right to coin.

form, there can be no judgment without some recognition of a difference between psychical occurrences and the system of reality. That is to say, there is no judgment unless the judging mind is more or less aware that it is possible to have an idea which is not in accordance with reality.

Thus, *if* an animal has no real world distinct from his train of mental images, if, that is, and just because, these are his world directly, and without discord, he cannot judge. The question is, *e. g.* when he seems disappointed, whether the pleasant image [1] simply disappears and a less pleasant image takes its place, or whether the erroneous image was distinguished as an element in " a mere idea," which could be retained and compared with the systematised perceptions which force it out, *as* an idea with reality.

We must all of us have seen a dog show signs of pleasure when he notices preparations for a walk, and then express the extreme of unhappiness when the walk is not taken at all, or he is left at home. People interpret these phenomena very carelessly. They say "he thought that he was going to be taken out." If he did "*think that*, etc," then he made a judgment. This would imply that he distinguishes between the images suggested to his mind, and the reality of their content as the future event of going out, and knew that he might have the one without the other following. But of

---

[1] It will be observed that we are not treating the mental images as being taken for such by the primitive mind. It is just in as far as they are *not* yet *taken for such* that they *are merely such*. Mr. James says that the first sensation is for the child the universe (*Psychology,* II. 7). But it is a universe in which all is equally mere fact, and there is no distinction of truth and falsehood, or reality and unreality. That can only come when an existent is found to be a fraud.

course it is quite possible that the dog has no distinct expectation of something different from his present images, but merely derives pleasure from them, which he expresses, and suffers and expresses pain when they are replaced by something else. It is here, no doubt, in the conflict of suggestion and perception, that judgment originates.

On the other hand, animals, especially domestic animals, do seem to use the imperative, which perhaps implies that they know what they want, and have it definitely contrasted with their present ideas as something to be realised.

However this may be, the claim of truth marks the minimum of Judgment. There can be no judgment until we distinguish psychical fact from the reference to Reality. A mere mental fact as such is not true or false. In other words, there is no judgment unless there is something that, formally speaking, is capable of being denied. When your dog sees you go to the front door, he may have an image of hunting a rabbit suggested to his mind, but so far there is nothing that can be denied. If he has the image, of course he has. There is nothing that can be denied until the meaning of this image is treated as a further fact beyond the image itself, in a system independent of the momentary consciousness in his mind. *Then* it is possible to say, " No, the fact does not correspond to your idea," *i. e.* what we are ultimately obliged to think as a system is inconsistent with the idea as you affirmed it of the same system.

(ii.) The first thing then in Judgment is that we must have a world of reality distinguished from the course of our ideas. Thereupon the claim to truth is actually made by attaching the meaning of an idea to some point in the real By what means the claim to truth is made.

world. This can only be done where an identity is recognised between reality and our meaning.

Thus (keeping to the Judgment of Perception) I say, "This table is made of oak." This table is given in perception already qualified by numberless judgments; it is a point in the continuous system or tissue which we take as reality. Among its qualities it has a certain grain and colour in the wood. I know the colour and grain of oak-wood, and if they are the same as those of the table, then the meaning or content "made of oak" coalesces with this point in reality, and instead of merely saying, "This table is made of wood that has such and such a grain and colour," I am able to say "This table is made of oak-wood."

This example shows the true distinction between the Logical Subject and Predicate. The fact is, that the ultimate subject in Judgment is always Reality. Of course the logical subject may be quite different from the grammatical subject. Some kinds of words cannot in strict grammar be made subjects of a sentence, though they can represent a logical subject quite well: *e. g.* "*Now* is the time." "*Here* is the right place." Adverbs, I suppose, cannot be grammatical subjects. But in these sentences they stand for the logical subjects, certain points in the perceptive series.

The true logical subject then is always reality, however much disguised by qualifications or conditions. The logical predicate is always the meaning of an idea; and the claim to be true consists in the affirmation of the meaning as belonging to the tissue of reality at the point indicated by the subject. The connection is always made by identity of content at the point where the idea joins the reality, so that *the judgment always appears as a revelation of something which is in reality.* It simply develops, accents, or gives accuracy to a recognised quality of the real. This is easily seen in cases of simple quality—*e. g.* " This colour is sky-blue." The colour is given, and the judgment merely identifies it with sky-blue, and so reveals another element belonging to its identity, the element of being seen in the sky on a clear day.

The analysis is not quite so easy when there is a concrete subject like a person ; for how can there be an identity between a person and a fact ? " A. B. passed me in the street this afternoon." Between what elements is the identity in this case? It is between him, as an individual whom I know by sight in other places, and him as he appeared this afternoon in particular surroundings. His identity already extends through a great many different particulars of time and place, and this judgment merely recognises one more particular as included in the same continuous history. " He in this context belongs to him in a former context." In this simple case the operative identity is probably that of my friend's personal appearance ; but the judgment is not merely about that but about his whole personality, of which his personal appearance is merely taken as a sign.

Any assertion which is incredible because the identical quality is wanting will illustrate the required structure. There is a story commented on by Thackeray in one of his occasional papers, which implied that the Duke of Wellington took home note-paper from a club to which he did not belong. (Thackeray gives the true explanation of the fact on which the suggestion was founded.) The identity concerned in this case would be that of character. Can we find an identity between the character involved in a piece of meanness like that suggested and the character of the Duke of Wellington? No; and *prima facie* therefore the judgment is false. The identity which should bind it together breaks it in two. But yet, again : supposing the external evidence to be strong enough, we may have to accept a fact which conflicts with a man's character as we conceive it. That is so : in such a case one kind of identity appears to contradict the other. I may think that I saw a man with my own eyes, doing something which wholly contradicts his character as I judge it. Then there is a conflict between identity in personal appearance and identity in character, and we have to criticise the two estimates of identity—*i. e.* to refer them both to our general system of knowledge, and to accept the connection which can be best adapted to that system.

We have got, then, as the active elements in Judgment a Subject in Reality, the meaning of an idea, and an identity between them.

Is this enough? Have we the peculiar act of affirmation wherever we have these conditions?

This is not the question by what elements of *language* the judgment is rendered. We shall speak of that in the next lecture. The question is now, simply, "Is a significant idea, referred to reality, always an assertion?"

The first answer seems to be that such an idea is always *in* an assertion, but need not constitute the whole of an assertion. If we think of a subject in judgment which is represented by a relative sentence, it seems clear that any idea which can stand a predicate can also form a part of a subject. " The exhibition which it is proposed to hold at Chicago in 1893 "—has in effect just the same elements of meaning, and just the same reference to a point in our world of reality as if the sentence ran, "It is proposed to hold an exhibition at Chicago in 1893." In common parlance we should say, that in the former case we entertain an idea—or conceive or represent it—while in the latter case we affirm it.

But if we go on to say that the former kind of sentence as truly represents the nature of thought as the latter, then it seems that we are mistaken. Even language does not admit such a clause to the rank of an independent sentence.

If we insist on considering it in its isolation, we probably eke it out in thought by an unarticulated affirmation such as that which constitutes an impersonal judgment ; in other words, we affirm it to belong to reality under some condition which remains unspecified. Thus the linguistic form of the relative clause, as also the separate existence of the spoken or written word, produces an illusion which has governed the greater part of logical theory so far as concerns the separation between concept and judgment, *i. e.* between entertaining ideas and affirming them in reality. In our waking life, all thought is judgment, every idea is referred to reality, and in being so referred, is ultimately affirmed of reality. The separation of elements in the texture of Judgment into Subjects and Predicates which, as separated, are conceived as *possible* Subjects and Predicates, is therefore theoretical and ideal, an analysis of a living tissue, not an enumeration of loose bricks out of which something is about to be built up.

(iii.) "Idea" has two principal meanings.

(α) A psychical presentation and

(β) An identical reference.

This distinction is the same as that between our course of ideas and our world of knowledge. We must try now to define it more accurately.

(α) An idea as a psychical presentation is strictly a particular. Every moment of consciousness is full of a given complex of presentation which passes away and can never be repeated without some difference. For this purpose a representation is just the same as a presentation; is, in fact, a presentation. Its detail at any given moment is filled in by the influence of the moment, and it can never occur again with precisely the same elements of detail as before. If we use the term "idea" in this sense, as a momentary particular mental state, it is nonsense to speak of having the same idea twice, or of referring it to a reality other than our mental life. The idea in this sense is a psychical image. We cannot illustrate this usage by any recognisable part of our mental furniture, for every such part which can be described and indicated by a general name, is something more than a psychical image. We can only say that that which at any moment we have in consciousness, when our waking perception encounters reality, is such an idea, and so too is the image supplied by memory, when considered simply as a datum, a fact, in our mental history.

(β) To get at the other sense of "idea" we should think

of the meaning of a word; a very simple case is that of a
proper name. What is the meaning of " St. Paul's Cathedral
in London"? No two people who have seen it have
carried away precisely the same image of it in their minds,
nor does memory, when it represents the Cathedral to each
of them, supply the same image in every detail and association twice over to the same person, nor do we for a
moment think that such an image *is* the Cathedral.[1] Yet
we neither doubt that the name *means* something, and that
the same to all those who employ it, nor that it means the
same to each of them at one time that it did at every other
time. The psychical images which formed the first vision
of it are dead and gone for ever, and so, after every occasion
on which it has been remembered, are those in which that
memory was evoked. The essence of the idea does not lie
in the peculiarities of any one of their varying presentations,
but in the identical reference that runs through them all,
and to which they all serve as material, and the content of
this reference *is* the object of our thought.

In order to distinguish and employ this reference it is
necessary that there should be a symbol for it, and so long
as it brings us to the object which is the centre of the
entire system, this symbol may vary within considerable
limits.

The commonest and most secure means of reference is

[1] When we are actually looking at the Cathedral, we say, " *That is*
the Cathedral." Does not this mean that we take our momentary
image, to which we point, to be the reality of the Cathedral ? Not
precisely so. It is the "that," not our definite predication about it,
which makes us so confident. The "that" is identified by our judgment,
but goes beyond it.

the word or name.[1] So confident are we in the "conventional" or artificially adapted character of this mark or sign
of reference, that we are inclined to treat it as absolutely
unvarying on every occasion of utterance. But of course
it is not unvarying. It differs in sound every time it is
spoken, and in context and appearance every time we see
it in a written shape. Our reliance upon it as identical
throughout depends on the fact that it has a recognisable
character to which its variations are irrelevant, and which
practically crushes out these variations from our attention.
Unless we are on the look-out for mispronunciations or
misprints, they do not interfere at all with our attention to
the main reference of words. We know that it is almost
impossible to detect misprints so long as one reads a book
with attention to its meaning. This then is a fair parallel
to the distinction which we are considering between two
kinds of ideas. If the momentary sound or look of a word
is analogous to idea as psychical presentation, "the word"
as a permanent possession of our knowledge is analogous
to the idea as a reference to an object in our systematic
world, and is the normal instrument of such a reference.

But either with the word or without it there may be a
symbol of another kind. Any psychical image that falls
within certain limits may appear as the momentary vehicle
of the constant reference to an object. Just as in recognising the reference of a word we omit to notice the accent
and loudness with which it is pronounced, or the quality of
the paper on which it is printed, just so in recognising the

---

[1] "A name is a sound which has significance according to convention," *i. e.* according to rational agreement.—*Ar. de Interp.* 16 a 19.

reference of a psychical image our attention fails to note its momentary context, colouring, and detail. If it includes something that definitely belongs to a systematic object in our world of objects, that is enough, unless counteracted by cross references, to effect the suggestion we require, and that, and nothing else, arrests our attention for the moment. When I think of St. Paul's Cathedral, it may be the west front, or the dome seen from the outside, or the gallery seen from the inside, that happens to occur to my mind; and further, that which does occur to me occurs in a particular form or colouring, dictated by the condition of my memory and attention at the moment. But these peculiarities are dwarfed by the meaning, and unless I consider them for psychological purposes, I do not know that they are there. It is the typical element only, the element which points to the common reference in which my interest centres, that forms the content of the idea in this sense, taken not as a transient feature of the mental complex, but as definitely suggesting a constant object in our constructed world. And it suggests this object because it, the typical element, is a common point that links together the various cases and the various presentations in which the object is given to us. In this sense it is a universal or an identity.

How can this conception of a logical idea be applied to a perfectly simple presentation? It would be impossible so to apply it, but there does not seem to be such a thing as a simple presentation in the sense of a presentation that has no connection as a universal with anything else. In the image of a particular blue colour, we cannot indeed separate out what makes it blue from what makes it the particular shade of blue that it is. But nevertheless its blueness makes it a symbol to us of blue in general, and when so thought of, crushes out of sight all the visible peculiarities that attend every spatial surface. We understand perfectly well that the colour is blue, and that in saying this we have gone beyond the limits of the momentary image, and have referred something in it as a universal quality to our world of objects. An idea, in this sense, is both less and more than a psychical image. It contains less, but stands for more. It includes only what is central and characteristic in the detail of each mental presentation, and therefore omits much. But it is not taken as a mental presentation at all, but as a content belonging to a systematic world of objects independent of my thought, and therefore stands for something which is not mere psychical image.

If therefore we are asked to display it as an image, as something fixed in a permanent outline, however pale or meagre, we cannot do so. It is not an abstract image, but a concrete habit or tendency. It can only be displayed in the judgment, that is, in a concrete case of reference to reality. Apart from this, it is a mere abstraction of analysis, a tendency to operate in a certain way upon certain psychical presentations. Psychically speaking, it is when realised in judgment a process more or less systematic, extending through time, and dealing with momentary presentations as its material. In other words, we may describe it as a selective rule, shown by its working, but not consciously before the mind—for if it were, it would no longer be an idea, but an idea of an idea.

Every judgment, whether made with language or without,

is an instance of such an idea, which may be called a
symbolic idea as distinct from a psychical image; "symbolic" because the mental units or images involved are not
as such taken as the whole of the object for which they
stand, but are in a secondary sense, as the word in a
primary sense, symbols or vehicles only.

Such ideas can have truth claimed for them, because they
have a reference beyond their mental existence. They
point to an object in a system of permanent objects, and
that to which they point may or may not suit the relation
which they claim for it. Therefore the judgment can only
be made by help of symbolic ideas. Mere mental facts,
occurrences in my mental history, taken as such, cannot
enter into judgment. When we judge about them, as in the
last sentence, they are not themselves subject or predicate,
but are referred to, like any other facts, by help of a
selective process dealing with our current mental images of
them. We shall not be far wrong then, if in every judgment,
under whatever disguises it may assume, we look for elements analogous to those which are manifest in the simple
perceptive judgment, "This is green," or "That is a horse."
The relation between these and more elaborate forms of
affirmation, such as the abstract judgment of science, has
partly been indicated in the earlier portion of this lecture.
The general definition of judgment has therefore been
sufficiently suggested on p. 72. Judgment is the reference
of a significant idea to a subject in reality, by means of an
identity of content between them.

THE PROPOSITION AND THE NAME

Judgment translated into Language.

1. JUDGMENT expressed in words is a Proposition. *Must* Judgment be expressed in words? We have assumed that this need not be so. Mill [1] says of Inference that "it is an operation which usually takes place by means of words, and in complicated cases can take place in no other way." The same is true of Judgment.

We may say in general that words are not needed, when thinking about objects by help of pictorial images will do the work demanded of the mind, *i. e.* when perfectly individualised connections in space and time are in question. Mr. Stout [2] gives chess-playing as an example. With the board before him, even an ordinary player does not need words to describe to himself the move which he is about to make.

Words are needed when we have to attend to the general plan of any system, as in thinking about organisms with reference to their type, or about political relations—about anything, that is, which is not of such a nature that the members of the idea can be symbolised in pictorial form. It would be difficult, for example, to comprehend the respiration of plants under a symbolic picture-idea drawn

---

[1] *Logic*, vol. i. c. i., init.   [2] In *Mind*, no. 62.

from the respiration of the higher animals. The relations which constitute a common element between the two processes do not include the movements, feelings, and visible changes in the circulatory fluid from which our image of animal respiration is chiefly drawn ; and we could hardly frame a pictorial idea that would duly insist on the chemical and organic conditions on which the common element of the process depends. In a case of this kind the word is the symbol which enables us to hold together in a coherent system, though not in a single image, the relations which make up the content of our thought.

"Words" may be of many different kinds—spoken, written, indicated by deaf and dumb signs ; all of these are derived from the word as it is in speech, although writing and printing become practically independent of sound, and we read, like the deaf and dumb alphabet, directly by the eye. Then there may be any kind of conventional signals either for letters, words, or sentences, and any kind of cipher or *memoria technica* either for private or for general use— in these the " conventional " nature of language reaches its climax, and the relation to a natural growth of speech has disappeared. And finally there are all forms of picture-writing, which need not, so far as its intrinsic nature goes, have any connection with speech at all, and which seems to form a direct transition between picture-thinking and thinking through the written sign.

All these must be considered under the head of language, as a fixed system of signs for meanings, before we can ultimately pronounce that we think without words.

Every Judgment, however, can be expressed in words

G

though not every Judgment need be so expressed or can readily be so.

Proposi-
tion and
sentence.

2. A Judgment expressed in words is a Proposition, which is one kind of sentence. A command question or wish is a sentence but not a proposition. A detached relative clause[1] is not even a complete sentence. The meaning of the imperative and the question seems to include some act of *will;* the meaning of a proposition is always given out simply for fact or truth. We need not consider any sentence that has no meaning at all.

Difference
between
Proposi-
tion and
Judgment.

3. Almost all English logicians speak of the Proposition and not of the Judgment.[2] This does not matter, so long as we are agreed about what they mean. They must mean the proposition *as understood*, and this is what we call the judgment.

In order to make this distinction clear, let us consider the proposition as it reaches us from without, that is to say, either as spoken or as written. The words, the parts of such a proposition, as we hear or read them, are separate and successive either in time alone, or in time and space. Further, the mere sounds or signs can be mastered apart from the meaning. You can repeat them or copy them without understanding them in the least, as *e. g.* in the case of a proposition in an unknown language. So far, the proposition has not become a judgment, and I do not suppose that any logician would admit that it deserved the name even of a proposition. But if not, then we must not confuse the attributes which it has before it becomes a proposition with those which it has after.

---

[1] See above, Lect. IV.

[2] So Mill, Venn, Jevons, Bain (see his note, p. 80).

Further, in understanding a proposition, or in construing a sentence into a proposition (if the sentence only becomes a proposition when understood), there are many degrees. I read upon a postcard, "A meeting will be held on Saturday next by the Women's Liberal Association, to discuss the taxation of ground-rents." The meaning of such a sentence takes time to grasp, and if the words are read aloud to us, must of necessity be apprehended by degrees. We understand very quickly that a meeting is to be held next Saturday. This understanding is already a judgment. It is something quite different from merely repeating the words which we read. It consists in realising them as meanings, and bringing these meanings together into a connected idea, and affirming this idea to belong to our real world. The meanings are not separate, outside one another, as the words are when we first hear or read them. They enter into each other, modify each other, and become parts of an ideal whole. This gradual apprehension of a sentence recalls to one the boyish amusement of melting down bits of lead in a ladle. At first the pieces all lie about, rigid and out of contact; but as they begin to be fused a fluid system is formed in which they give up their rigidity and independence, and enter into the closest possible contact, so that their movements and position determine each other. But still some parts, like words not yet grasped, remain hard and separate, and it is only when the melting is complete that this isolation is destroyed, and there are no longer detached fragments, but a fluid body such that all its parts are in the closest connection with one another.

Thus then in understanding a sentence we have a judgment from the first. The rest of the process of understanding consists in completing the content of this judgment by fusing with it the meanings of the words not yet apprehended ; and in the completeness with which this is effected there will always be great differences of degree between different minds, and also between the same mind at different times. Some of us attach a complete and distinct meaning to the words " Women's Liberal Association " ; some of us do not know, or have forgotten, exactly what it is, and what are its aims and history. All of us have some conception of the purpose described as " taxation of ground rents," but the phrase conveys a perfectly definite scheme hardly to one in a thousand readers. Nevertheless, in so far as we have some symbolic idea which refers to this place or context in the world of objects, the content of this idea enters into and modifies the total meaning which in apprehending the sentence before us we affirm of reality. The heard or written proposition (or sentence, if it is not a proposition till understood) serves as an instrument by which we build up in our intellectual world a sort of plan or scheme of connected meanings, and also, not subsequently but concurrently with this work of building, affirm the whole content thus being put together to be true of reality. Then we have what I call a Judgment. It is not that the words are necessarily forgotten ; they, or at least the principal significant terms, are probably still in the mind as guides and symbols ; but yet a constructive work has been done ; a complex experience has been called up and analysed, and its parts fitted together in a certain definite order by the operation of universal ideas or meanings, each of which is a system play-

ing into other systems ; and the whole thus realised has been
added as an extension to the significance of the continuous
judgment which forms our waking consciousness. The in-
convenience of the term "proposition" is that it tends to
confuse the heard or written sentence in its separate words
with the proposition as apprehended and intellectually
affirmed. And these two things have quite different
characteristics.

4. Thus we must be very careful how we apply the con- Parts of
ception of "parts of speech." The grammatical analysis Speech.
which classifies words as substantives, adjectives, adverbs,
verbs, and the like, is not to be taken as telling us what
words are by themselves, but just the opposite, viz. what
they do when employed in a significant sentence. They
are studied separately for convenience in attending to them,
as we may study the wheels and pistons of an engine ; but
the work which gives them their names can only be done
when they are together. This truth is often expressed by
saying that "the sentence is the unit of language," *i. e.* a
word taken by itself cannot have a complete meaning—
unless it is a verb, or used with verbal force, for a verb is
an unanalysed sentence. If any one uses a substantive or
adverb by itself, we think that he has not finished his sentence, and no meaning is conveyed to our minds. We ask
him, "Well, what about it ?" The same is true, as we saw,
of a relative clause. If we read in a newspaper such a
clause as this, "The epidemic of influenza, which has
appeared in England for three successive seasons," followed
by a full stop, we should infer, without hesitation, that some
words had dropped out by accident. Of course such a

combination of words would make us think something, but
the meaning which we might ascribe to it would be con-
jectural ; we should necessarily complete the thought for
ourselves by some affirmation—some relation to reality—
while recognising that no such relation was given in the
clause as we read it. Nothing less than a sentence, or,
omitting the wish and the command, nothing less than a
proposition, conveys a meaning in which the mind can
acquiesce as not requiring to be supplemented conjecturally.
There are traces in language that indicate the sentence to
have been historically prior to the word. I question whether
the word could be certainly distinguished within the sentence in early languages that have not been reduced to
writing. The tendency of reflective analysis, as in grammar
and dictionaries, is to give it a more and more artificial
isolation. The Greeks did not separate their words in
writing, and they wrote down the change in a terminal con-
sonant produced by the initial letter of the next word, just
as if it was within a compound word. Nor had they really
any current term co-extensive with our "word." Where we
should say "the word 'horse'" they most commonly use
the neuter article "the" followed by the word in question
as if in quotation-marks ("the 'horse'"). In defining noun
and verb, Aristotle has no simple class name like "word"
to employ as a common element of the definition, but uses
the curious description "a portion of discourse, of which no
part has a meaning by itself."

Of course, single words often stand as signs for propositions. It is interesting to note the pregnant meaning of a
single word in the mouth of a child. Thus "stool" was

used to mean "(1) Where is my stool? (2) My stool is broken; (3) Lift me on to the stool; (4) Here is a stool."[1] There is in this an interesting conflict of form and meaning, owing to the child of European race having at command only "parts of speech." In a less analytical language he might have at command a sound corresponding to a sentence rather than to a "noun substantive."

The verb of inflected languages,[2] such as Greek or Latin, in which the "nominative case" need not be supplied even by a pronoun, is the type for us of a sentence not yet broken up.

The bearing of this truth on Logic is to make us treat it in two parts and not in three. We do not treat of Name, Proposition, Syllogism, or of Concept, Judgment, Inference, but only of the two latter parts. The name or concept has no reality in living language or living thought, except when referred to its place in a proposition or judgment. We ought not to think of propositions as built up by putting words or names together, but of words or names as distinguished though not separable elements in propositions. Aristotle takes the simple and straightforward view. "A term is the element into which a proposition is broken up, such as subject and predicate."[3] Of course different languages separate the parts of the proposition very differently,

---

[1] Preyer, quoted in *Höffding. Psych.*, 176.

[2] In German and English, though the verb is inflected, custom forbids it to stand without the pronoun.

[3] *Anal. prior.*, 24b, 16. The opposite view seems to be expressed in the beginning of the περὶ Ἑρμηνείας, that the separate word corresponds to the separate idea. I have attempted to explain this as an illusion, p. 73, above.

and uneducated people hardly separate them at all. Formal Logic breaks down the grammatical meaning of "name," so far as to treat as a "logical name" any complex words that can stand as Subject or Predicate in a Proposition (*e. g.* a relative clause).

Denotation and Connotation.

5. The doctrine of the meaning of names has suffered from their relation to propositions not being borne in mind. Mill's discussion [1] is very sensible, but, as always, very careless of strict system. More especially it seems a pity to state the question as if it concerned a division of names into Connotative and Non-connotative; because in this way we from the first let go of the idea that the meaning of a name has necessarily two aspects,[2] and we almost bind ourselves to make out that there are some non-connotative names. It is better to consider this latter subject on its merits. Mill says that an ordinary significant name such as "man" "signifies the subjects directly, the attributes indirectly; it *denotes* the subjects, and implies or involves or indicates, or, as we shall say henceforth, *connotes*, the attributes." In short, the denotation of a name consists of the things *to which* it *ap*plies, the connotation consists of the properties which it *im*plies. The denotation is made up of individuals and the connotation of attributes. Denotation is also called Extension, especially if we are speaking of Concepts rather than of names. Connotation is then called Intension. In the German writers it is more usual to say that the Extension or Area (*Umfang*) consists not of the individuals, but of the species that are contained in

---

[1] *Logic*, Bk. I. c. ii. § 5. Cf. Venn, 174 and 183, and Bain, 48.

[2] See Bradley, p. 155.

the meaning of a general name. They oppose it to Content (*Inhalt*), corresponding to our "Connotation." Thus the " Area " of " rose " would not be the individual roses in the world, but rather all the species of rose in the world (*Rosa Canina*, *Rosa Rubiginosa*, etc.). This raises a difficulty as to the denotation of a specific name, but perhaps represents the actual process of thought, in the case of a generic name, better than that which Mill adopts. The difference is not important.

Well, then, according to Mill, when we say, " The Marshal Niel is a yellow rose," we refer directly to a group of real or possible objects, and we mean that all these individual objects are yellow roses. The attributes are only mentioned by the way, or implied. So Dr. Venn says that the denotation is real, and the connotation is notional.

But there is another side to this question. The objects may be *what you mean*, but the attributes seem to be *the meaning*, for how can you (especially on Mill's theory of the proposition) refer to any objects except through these attributes, unless indeed you can point to them with your finger ? And so again it seems, especially if we consider Mill's account of predication, as if the Connotation were the primary meaning and the Denotation the secondary meaning. The Connotation determines the Denotation ; and if we " define" the meaning of the name it is the Connotation that we state. And so Mill tells us two or three pages further on, that whenever the names given to objects have properly any meaning, the meaning resides not in what they denote, but in what they connote. In short, the denotation of a general name is simply the meaning of its plural, or of its singular, in that sense in which it implies a plural, while the connotation is the meaning *per se*, not considered in its instances.

It is clear then that every name has these two kinds of meaning—first, a content, and then instances, whether possible or actual, of the content; and the two are obviously inseparable, although they are distinguishable. Ultimately, indeed, the denotation itself is an attribute, and so part of the connotation. It is one of the attributes of man to be a unit in the plurality men, *i. e.* to be "a man." It may be said that some names have no plural. If so, these would be non-denotative rather than non-connotative, but in fact this is not true. The content of a significant name can always, unless hindered by a special convention (see below on proper names), be *prima facie* regarded, in respect of its actual embodiment, as a unit against other possible units. Granting that there may be an object, which according to our knowledge can only be real as an isolated case, the very consideration of it as such a case is enough to distinguish its existence, whether real or possible, from its content. Thus, as a real or possible existence, the object is *ipso facto* considered in the light of a particular, and as capable of entering into a plurality. But its nature or content, the meaning of its name, cannot enter into a plurality. Two *meanings*, two connotations, are alternative and irreconcilable. Denotation and connotation are thus simply the particular, or particulars, which embody or are thought of as embodying a content, and the single or universal content itself.

6. Therefore I think that Mill is wrong, when he goes on, "The only names of objects which connote nothing are Proper Names, and these have, strictly speaking, no signifi-cation." [1] If the name has no signification, for what reason, or by what means, is it attached to a person or a place? You may say that it is only a conventional mark. But a mark which has power to select from all objects in the world, and bring to our minds, a particular absent object, is surely a significant mark. Granted that it is conventional, yet by what mechanism, and for what purpose, does the convention operate?

Mill's point, however, is quite clear. To be told the name of a person or object does not inform us of his or its attributes. Directly, it only warns us by what sign the same person or object will be recognisable in language again.[2] If a name is changed, the new name tells us nothing different from the old,[3] whereas if an object that was called vegetable is now called animal, our conception of it is radically trans-formed. A name expresses the continued identity of an object, and this implies only a historical continuity of attri-butes and relations, and no constant attribute whatever.

[1] Cf. Venn, 183 ff, and Bradley, 156.

[2] We cannot make it a distinctive mark of proper names that they recur in different and quite disconnected meanings, because the words which are used as general names have this same property. Nor can we say that a proper name is not used in the same sense of more than one object. Family names and national names make this plainly untrue. Through these, and names typically employed, there is a clear gradation from proper to general names.

[3] The case of marriage may be urged. But a lady's change of name does not by itself indicate marriage. It is a mere fact, which may have various explanations. The change of title (from "Miss" to "Mrs.") is more significant, but it is not a change of name.

Thus a *proper* name is a contradiction in terms.[1] A name should have a meaning. But a meaning cannot be proper—that is, particular. The name-word is therefore like a demonstrative pronoun, if this were attached, by a special convention, to one identifiable object only. It acquires meaning, but its meaning is an ever-growing contradiction with its usage. The meaning is necessarily general, the usage is *ex hypothesi* particular.

This convention of usage, which prevents a proper name from becoming general, *i. e.* from being cut loose and used simply for its meaning, is always on the point of breaking down.[2] Christian names usually indicate sex ; family names, though now with little certainty, descent and relationship. There are germs of a general meaning within the several usages of names ; while a Solon, a Crœsus, a Christian, a Mahometan, have become purely general names cut loose from all unique reference. Still in a proper name, as such, we have no right to build on any general meaning. Recognition is its only purpose ; and the law permits, it has been said, that a man should have one name for Mondays, Wednesdays, and Fridays, and another for Tuesdays, Thursdays, and Saturdays. The essence of a name is a reference to unique identity ; it employs meaning only to establish identity.

What kinds of things have proper names given, then ? Always things *individually* known to the people who give

---

[1] So, from the complementary point of view, is a *general* name. A name, it may be urged, *is* meant to designate a particular thing or things. And this a name with a true "meaning" cannot do.

[2] See note on last page.

the name, and interesting to them for some reason beyond
generic or specific qualities. Pet animals have names,
when other animals of the same kind have not. The
peasants throughout England use names, it is said, for all
the fields, although strangers are not usually acquainted
with them.

A Proper Name, then, has a connotation, but not a
fixed general connotation. It is attached to a unique
individual, and connotes whatever may be involved in
his identity, or is instrumental in bringing it before the
mind.

When we think of history, the importance of proper
names becomes very great. This is the characteristic logical
difference between history and science. "England" and
"France" are proper names, names of individual existences
in contact with our world of perception, not scientific ab-
stractions. Even the words, "1892 A.D.," are partly of the
nature of a proper name. They say nothing merely general
or abstract about this year; they assign the year a name by
counting forwards from a unique point in the series of years,
itself designated by the name of a historical personage.
Everything that is simply distinguished by its place in the
series of events in space and time is in some degree a proper
name. Thus we could not identify the French Revolution
by mere scientific definition. It is known by its proper
name, as a unique event, in a particular place and time.
When thus identified it may have all kinds of general ideas
attached to it. It would be hard to show that "Our earth,"
"Our solar system" are not proper names, in virtue of their
uniqueness.

Inverse
ratio of
Connota-
tion and
Denota-
tion.

7. It has sometimes been said that Connotation is in inverse ratio [1] to Denotation. Mill explains the fact upon which any such idea rests.[2] If we arrange things in classes, such that the one class includes the other—*e. g. Species* "Buttercup," *Genus* "Ranunculus," *Order* "Ranunculaceæ," —of course the genus will contain many species besides the one mentioned, and the order many genera besides the one mentioned. The object of the arrangement is that they should do so, and thus bring out the graduated natural affinities which prevail in the world. Thus the denotation of the genus-name is larger than that [3] of the species, and the denotation of the order-name is larger than that of the genus-name.

But further, in such an arrangement the genus can contain only the attributes which are common to all the species, and the order can contain only the attributes which are common to all the genera ; so the genus-name implies fewer attributes (less connotation) than any one species-name under it, and the order-name implies fewer attributes (less connotation) than any one genus-name under it.

That is the fact which suggests the conception of Denotation and Connotation as varying inversely.

But in any case it would not be right to speak thus mathematically of an inverse ratio, because there is no meaning in a numerical comparison of attributes and indi-

---

[1] See Venn, p. 174, for reference to Hamilton. Venn points out the fallacy.

[2] *Logic*, Bk. I. ch. vii. § 5.

[3] Or "than the species," if we take the denotation as made up of species.

viduals, and the addition of one attribute will exclude sometimes more and sometimes fewer individuals.[1]

And there are more important objections to the whole
idea of a corresponding gradation in these two kinds of
meaning. The idea of abstraction thus implied is altogether
wrong. The meaning of a genus-name does not *omit* the
properties in which the species differ. If it did, it would
omit nearly all properties. What happens is that the genus-
idea represents the general plan on which the species are
built, but provides for each of the parts that constitute the
whole, varying in the specific cases within certain limits.
Thus in the Ranunculaceæ some species have no petals.
But we do not omit the character "petals" from the genus-
idea. We state the general plan so far as this element is
concerned as "Petals five or more ; rarely none." This is
read by a botanist to mean that in some groups the petals
tend to be aborted, and sometimes are actually missing. In
a symbolic representation of the genus-idea such a property
may stand as A, and its various specific forms as A_1, A_2,
A_3, etc. There is nothing to prevent these specific phases
approaching and sometimes reaching zero. No doubt if
the classification is pursued in the direction of "universals"
containing fewer and fewer properties, it is possible to arrive
at concepts which appear to have a larger denotation and a
smaller connotation than those "below" them. "Ranunculaceæ," "Dicotyledons," "Plants," "Organisms."

But this is only because we choose to form our system by
that process of abstraction which consists in leaving out
properties. *E. g.* comparing Frenchmen with men in general,

[1] See Jevons, p. 40.

we assume that "Frenchman" indicates (α) all the qualities of humanity as such, and (β) the qualities of French humanity in addition to these. But is this so in fact? Humanity, considered as a wider, and therefore as a deeper, idea, may have more content, as well as more area, than Frenchmanity. We do not really, in thinking of humanity, omit from our schematic thought all references to qualities of Greek, Jew, English, and German, and their bearing and interaction upon one another. It is only that we have been drilled to assume a certain neatness in the pyramidal arrangement by which we vainly try to reduce the meaning of a great idea to something that has no system and no inter-relation of parts, but approaches as near as possible in fixity to the character of a definite image, though far removed from such a character in the impossibility of bringing it before the mind.

So we can only say, "the greater the denotation the less the connotation," and *vice versâ*, in as far as we arrange ideas by progressive abstraction in the sense of progressive omission. But it is not the only way of regarding them. Things may develop new inter-relations as their number increases. Has the community, as Mr. Bradley asks, less meaning than the individual person? But we must not consider the community, would be the answer; we must simply consider the relation of an idea of one individual to any idea that applies to many individuals. This is simply to rule out those relations that arise within progressively larger wholes. We can do so, if we think the exclusion necessary in the interests of logical purity, but it is only by doing so that we can maintain the traditional view of connotation and denotation. It is worth while to think out the matter for ourselves in relation to such familiar ideas as those of man and animal. It is plain that the idea of "animal" cannot omit all reference to intelligence, but must in some way allow for the different phases of this property which run throughout the animal kingdom, and only find a climax in man. And it is plain also, that even if intelligence were wholly omitted, this would not leave behind, as in a simple stratification, properties in which the whole animal kingdom was the same. Man's animality is modified throughout in a way corresponding to his rationality, so that no general idea could be framed including him and other animals, simply by collecting properties which are the same and omitting those which are different. The idea of "man" really becomes richer when considered in the light of a comparison [1] with the rest of the animal world. Our great systems of natural classification, representing affinities graduated by descent, are what give the view which we have criticised a certain objective importance. But they do not establish it as an exclusive logical doctrine.

[1] If we insist on throwing the whole of this comparison, in explicit shape, into the complete idea of man, then the progress to the idea "animal" can add nothing ; even so, however, it loses nothing, but simply becomes the same set of relations, looked at, so to speak, from the other end.

LECTURE VI

PARTS OF THE JUDGMENT, AND ITS UNITY

Parts of the Judgment.

1. THE result of taking the Judgment as one with the Proposition has been to assume that its parts were the same as those of the Proposition; [1] and moreover the same as those of the Proposition in a very artificial form, viz. as analysed into three separable elements, "Subject," "Predicate," "Copula," commonly represented in the examples of the text-books by Substantive, Adjective or Substantive, and the Verb "is."

For the operation of Formal Logic it is almost necessary to have these parts, because it is requisite to transpose the terms (as in Conversion) without changing their meaning,[2] and to get rid of *tenses*, which do not belong to Scientific Judgment, and are very troublesome in Formal Inference.

Thus in Formal Logic we prefer the shape of sentence "Gold is lustrous" to "Gold glitters," and "The bridge is

---

[1] This assumption involves (see Lecture V.) a confusion between the Proposition as thoroughly understood, and the Proposition as a series of partially significant sounds or signs. For obvious reasons, this confusion is very readily made.

[2] If the "predicate" is a Substantive, this presents no difficulty; and if it is an Adjective, it can be done by a little straining of grammar, or the insertion of "thing" or "things." With a verb it is more clumsy.

cracked" to "There is a crack in the bridge." And practically all propositions can be thrown into this shape, which
is convenient for comparing them. The educational value
of elementary formal logic consists chiefly, I am convinced,
in the exercise of paraphrasing poetical or rhetorical assertions into this typical shape, with the least possible sacrifice
of meaning. The commonest mistakes in the work of
beginners, within my experience as a teacher, consist
in failures to interpret rightly the sentence given for
analysis.

But this type is not really ultimate. The judgment can
be conveyed without a grammatical subject, and without
the verb " is "—indeed without any grammatical verb at all.
On the whole this agrees with Mill's view in the chapter
"Of Propositions." [1] He points out (§ 1) that we really
need nothing but the Subject and Predicate, and that the
copula is a mere sign of their connection *as* Subject and
Predicate. He does not, however, discuss the case in which
the grammatical Subject is absent.

2. In analysing the Judgment as an act of thought we Copula
may begin by dismissing the separate Copula. It has no
separate existence in thought corresponding to its separate
place in the typical proposition of Formal Logic. It has
come to be considered separately, because the abstract verb
"is" is used in our languages as a sign of the complete
enunciation. But there is not in the Judgment any separate
significant idea—any third idea—coming in between the
Subject and Predicate of Judgment. We should try to
think of the Copula not as a link, separable and always

---

[1] Mill's *Logic*, Bk. I. ch. iv.

intrinsically the same,[1] connecting two distinct things. We should think of it rather as the grip with which the parts of a single complex whole cohere with one another, differing according to the nature of the whole and the inter-dependence of its parts. Benno Erdmann[2] has strikingly expressed this point of view by saying, that in the Judgment, "The dead ride fast," the Subject is "the dead," the Predicate "fast riding," *and the Copula "the fast riding of the dead."* In other words, the Copula is simply the Judgment considered exclusively as a cohesion between parts of a complex idea, the individual connection between which can only be indicated by supplying the idea of those parts themselves.

Are Subject and Predicate necessary?

3. The explicit Predicate is more necessary than the explicit Subject.

We have spoken of Judgments expressed by one word, "Fire!" "Thieves!" etc., and also of impersonal Propositions, "It is raining," "It is thawing." These two classes of Judgments show hardly any explicit Subject at all. But we could not assert anything without a Predicate—that would be to assert without asserting anything in particular.

As these Judgments have, roughly speaking, a Predicate and no Subject, I do not think it convenient to call them, with Dr. Venn, existential judgments. It is true that they refer to reality, but their *peculiarity* is in not referring to a distinct subject. And when used for definite and complex assertions they become very artificial, *e. g.* "There is a

---

[1] In a comic Logic, with pictures, meant to stimulate dull minds at a University, I have seen the Copula represented as the coupling-link between two railway carriages. This is an excellent type of the way in which we should *not* think of it.

[2] *Logik*, p. 189.

British Constitution by which our liberties are guaranteed."
Instead of organising the content of the Judgment, such a
form of assertion simply tosses the whole of it into the
Predicate in a single mass.

The question is only one of words ; but it appears to me
more convenient to reserve the term Existential judgments
for those highly artificial assertions which actually employ
the Predicate " exist " or " existence," *e. g.* " Matter exists."
These are at the opposite end of the scale from those last-
mentioned, and are the nearest approach to Judgment with
Subject and no Predicate. That is to say, their Predicate
is the generalised abstract form of predication [1] without any
special content—the kind and degree of existence asserted
being understood from the context.

Except, however, in the case of these peculiarly abstract
and reflective assertions, it must be laid down that a predicated content is necessary to judgment, while an *explicit*
subject of predication is unnecessary.

4. If it is possible, in some cases, to throw the whole Two Ideas
content of judgment into the predicate, this rather disposes or Things.
us to criticise the notion that there must be two distinct
matters, objects, ideas, or contents, in every judgment.
The notion in question has two forms.

It is thought that the Judgment consists in putting two
ideas together,[2] or,

---

[1] Expressed in Greek by the word corresponding to " is," used with
an accent, which does not belong to it in its ordinary use. He is good
= ἀγαθός ἐστι ; He exists = ἔστι.

[2] For this conception, see Hamilton's *Lectures on Logic*, i. 227, and
for a criticism on it, Mill's *Logic*, Bk. I. ch. v., *init*. Mr. Venn seems
to incline to Hamilton's view, but I do not feel sure that he intends to

That the Judgment consists in comparing two or more things.[1]

Two Ideas. (a) The notion of "two ideas" has two principal difficulties.

Notion of mental transition pure and simple. (i.) In its simplest shape the notion of "two ideas" involves the great blunder which I explained in Lecture IV. It suggests that the parts of Judgment are separate and successive psychical states, and that the Judgment consists in a change from the one to the other. Herbert Spencer, as I understand him, considers every relation to be apprehended as a mental change or passage from one idea to another. This view would degrade logical connection into mere psychical transition. I do not say that there is no psychical transition in Judgment. I do say that psychical transition is not enough to make a Judgment. The parts of Judgment, as we saw in the last lecture, do not succeed one another separately like the parts of a sentence. The relation between Subject and Predicate is not a relation between mental states, but is itself the content of a single though continuous mental state. Mill has rightly touched on this point. "When I say that fire causes heat, do I mean that my idea of fire causes my idea of heat?"[2] and so on. The fact is that "Fire-causing-heat" is itself the single content or meaning represented in my symbolic idea; it is not a succession of psychical states in my mind, or a passage from the idea of fire to the idea of causing heat.

discuss the question in the form in which it is referred to in the text. See his *Empirical Logic*, pp. 210 and 211.

[1] See Jevons, pp. 61-2; and Mill, Bk. I. ch. iii., *init.*; and ch. iv., *init.*

[2] *Logic*, Bk. I. ch. v. § 1.

(ii.) But further, understanding now that the Judgment is composed of a single ideal content, and is not a transition from one mental state to another, there is still a difficulty in the conception that its component elements are nothing but ideas. If the Subject in Judgment is no more than an ideal content, how, by what means, does the Judgment claim to be true of Reality? "The Subject cannot belong to the content or fall within it, for in that case it would be the idea attributed to itself."[1] If the Subject were only a part of an ideal content it would not claim to be true of Reality, and where it *appears* to be only an ideal content there is much dispute in what sense the Judgment does claim to be true of Reality. "Violations of a law of nature are impossible." "The three angles of a triangle are equal to two right angles." "All trespassers will be prosecuted." In these Judgments we should find it hard to make out that the Subjects are real things corresponding to our ideas. And yet, if they are not, how can the Judgment attach itself to Reality? This is the difficult question of the distinction between the categorical and the hypothetical Judgment, and we shall have to return to it. In the meantime, we must adhere to our judgment of perception as the true underlying type. The Subject is here not an idea, but is the given reality, *this* or *that*, and the Judgment is not a conjunction of two ideas, but is present reality qualified by an idea. We say, "It is very hot," meaning that heat, the general quality embodied for us in an ideal content, is true of— forms one tissue with—the surroundings which here and now press upon our attention. Or again, "This is red,"

[1] Bradley's *Principles of Logic*, p. 14.

i. e. the content of the idea red is what my attention selects and emphasises within the mass of detail presented to it in its own unique focus which the pronoun "this" simply points out as though with the finger. We shall find such a structure underlying all the more artificial forms of Judgment.

Two Things.

(β) Thus it would seem that Jevons and Mill are much nearer the real point when they say that the proposition has to do with two Things, or with a Thing and a group of Things. But we must notice in passing that Mill,[1] after fighting hard against calling them Ideas, takes our breath away by saying that they are states of consciousness. There is, of course, a difficulty, which I will not try to deal with now, in the fact that however much we *refer* to things, we have nothing to *work with intellectually* but our ideas of them, and in some types of Judgment the reference to real things is difficult to trace. Mill further emphasises this by showing, that what we assert in ordinary *general* Judgment is co-existence of attributes.[2] "Now when we say, Man is mortal, we mean that wherever these various mental and physical phenomena (the attributes of man) are all found, then we have assurance that the other physical and mental phenomenon called death, will not fail to take place." That is, no doubt, a very indirect way of referring to the real things which we call men. Moreover, he treats all conclusions in geometry and mechanics as hypothetical.[3] All this we shall have to return to, in order to reconcile it with our doctrine ; which is apparently coincident with

[1] *Logic*, Bk. I. ch. v. § 5.   [2] *Ibid.*, § 4.
[3] *Ibid.*, Bk. II. ch. vi. §§ 3, 4.

Mill's view in the place first alluded to, that the subject in Judgment is always reality.

But our point at present is only the duality ascribed to the Judgment by saying that it essentially deals with *two* things or groups of things. Jevons even says [1] that every Judgment is a comparison of two things—though these "things" are really, it would seem, groups of things.[2] We thus have it impressed upon our minds that there is one "thing" corresponding to the Subject-word (or clause) of the Propositional sentence, and another "thing" corresponding to the Predicate-word (or clause), and that these are somehow separate, like two railway carriages, till we bring them together by the coupling-link of the copula. This is a very inconvenient way of looking at the matter. It is not true that all Judgment is comparison, in the proper and usual sense of the word. It is not true that Judgment involves two things; two or more things may be mentioned in a Judgment, but they cannot correspond respectively to the Subject and Predicate. It is a real Comparison if you say, "A.B. is taller than C.D.," but C.D. is here not a term in the Judgment. The one person, A.B., is qualified by the ideal content "taller than C.D.," and the idea of A.B. so qualified is referred to, or discriminated within, perceptive reality. Comparison is a rather complex process, and consists in a cross-reference by which each of two objects is judged according to a standard furnished by the other ; but this complex process is not necessary to all Judgment, and cannot be expressed with complete convenience in a single Judgment. And in

---

[1] *Elementary Lessons in Logic*, p. 61.   [2] *Ibid.*, p. 62.

any case the two objects that enter into the comparison do not correspond to two essential parts of Judgment.

It is far more simple and true to say that Judgment is always the analysis *and* synthesis of elements in some one thing or ideal content. "Gold is yellow" has not within it, as Jevons says it has,[1] any direct comparison of gold with other yellow substances. It simply drags to light the property "yellow" as distinct within the complex of attributes belonging to gold, while at the same time insisting that this property—this meaning of an idea—belongs to, is of one piece with, perceived reality in so far as gold is given in such reality. The Judgment exhibits the content in its parts. It breaks it up, and pronounces it to be all of one tissue, by one and the same indivisible act. We should practically have a much fairer chance of seeing clearly what Judgment is if we began by considering it as not two things or two terms—but as one thing or one term drawn out into elements by discriminating selection. Even if the paradox that every "Thing" is a Judgment neglects some necessary distinctions, I am convinced that we shall understand Judgment much more clearly if we do our best to approach it from this point of view. Whenever we look or listen, and *notice* features and qualities in the perceptions that arrest the eye and ear, we are rapidly and continuously judging. "The fire is crackling," "The daylight is waning," "That bookshelf is not full," "The window-curtain is twisted." In none of these cases is there any separation other than an intellectual distinction between the predicated content and the perceived reality. The Judgment is simply a distinct

---

[1] *Loc. cit.*

insistence on a quality within a certain focus of reality as belonging to that reality. This is the fundamental nature of Judgment.

Therefore, to draw our conclusion as to the Unity of the Judgment, it is not a transition from one mental state to another; the relation of which it consists is not between ideas in it, but is the content of the idea which forms it. Judgment is not primarily comparison between two things; it is a thing or content displayed as possessing some definite relation or quality within its identity. Every Judgment is the content of one idea, but you may of course distinguish relations between ideal elements within this idea. " Fire causes heat " is a single content or idea, the nature of fire, expanded into one of its properties.

5. But then, if the whole Judgment is a single content, Distinc- what is the difference between Subject and Predicate, and is tion be- tween Sub- it necessary to distinguish Subject from Predicate at all? ject and Predicate. If *some* Judgments can be made without explicit Subjects, cannot *all* be made in that way ?

This suggestion is very useful as carrying on the simplest type of Judgment throughout the whole theory of Judgment. By a little torture of expression any Judgment can be thrown into a form in which undefined Reality is the general subject, and the whole mass of the Judgment is the Predicate. " William Pitt was a great statesman " = " There was a great statesman named William Pitt " ; " The three angles of every triangle are equal to two right angles " = " There are figures known as triangles with their three angles equal to two right angles " ; " All citizens are members of a moral order " = " There is a moral order, including the

relations of citizenship"; "All trespassers will be prosecuted" = "Here are conditions which ensure the prosecu-
tion of possible trespassers." Or you might always put a
subject, "Reality is such that"—"Reality is characterised
by."

Thus we see that, as we have said before, in every Judgment the ultimate subject is Reality, the world in contact
with us as we have already qualified it by previous Judgment.
It is a less mistake to reject the Subject and Predicate in
the Judgment altogether, than to think that they are separate
things or ideas, and that in judging you pass or change from
one to the other. Always bear in mind that it is possible
to mass the whole Judgment as a single Predicate directly or
indirectly true of Reality.

Having said this much, to make the Unity of the Judgment unmistakable, we may now safely distinguish between
the Subject and Predicate in the Judgment. And we shall
find the safest clue to be that the explicit Subject, when
there is one, marks the place at which, or the conditions
under which, Reality accepts the Predicate. The natural
Subject is concrete, and the Predicate abstract ; the Subject
real, and the Predicate ideal, but pronounced to be real.
The reason of this is that every Judgment is the connection
of parts in a whole, and to be a whole is the characteristic
of reality. In other words, the natural course of thought is
to define further what is already in great part defined, and
our real world is that which we have so far defined. The
isolated judgments of the text-books make it very hard to
grasp this, because you seem to begin anywhere for no
connected reason at all. But if we reflect on actual thought,

we find that, as Mr. Stout very cleverly says, we are always developing a "subject" which is in our minds (in the ordinary sense of a "subject of conversation"), and this subject is some region or province of the world of reality.

Now the explicit Subject in Judgment or the grammatical Subject in Proposition does not always set out the full nature of this, but merely some mark or point in it which we wish to insist upon. So that we may find in Judgment almost anything serving as explicit Subject. Thus, as Aristotle said quite plainly and sensibly, it is natural to say "The horse is white," but we *may* have occasion to say "This white is a horse"; it depends on the way in which the Subject comes into our minds.[1] Usually the Subject will be what Dr. Venn calls the heavier term, *i. e.* the term with more connotation. When there is no difference of concreteness between parts and whole, the Judgment becomes reversible as in the equation $7 + 5 = 12$. There is no distinction here between Subject and Predicate. The real underlying unity or Subject is the numerical system.

Therefore by recognising Subject and Predicate we represent the organisation of knowledge, and the connection of inherence or consequence within the content of our knowledge. If we do not recognise this distinction we throw the whole of Judgment into an undifferentiated mass of fact, running all assertion into the same mould, "It is the case that," etc. One difficulty still remains. If the relation between Subject and Predicate is within an idea, and not between ideas—that is, if the whole explicit content, Subject and

---

[1] See Prof. Bain, p. 56, upon the Universe, and Universe of Discourse, *i. e.* the general subject which you have in your mind.

Predicate together, can be regarded as predicated of reality, —why is the act of predication expressed by a verb, *i. e.* a sign of activity within this content? Why is a verb often if not always the form of predication which connotes Subject and Predicate? Not because it is a time-word. On the contrary, we want to get rid of the tense in Logic. The time of a Judgment ought to be determined only by the special connection between Subject and Predicate, not by tense, because tense is always subjective, merely relative to the time of speaking, and is accidental to the content of Judgment. Action seems nearer to what we want; the *verb* expresses both action and predicate. But the *idea* of action again does not make a predication, and the verb "is" does not *really indicate* action. Perhaps it is the demonstrative element in a finite verb that makes it the vehicle of predication, *i. e.* in a finite verb you have a meaning referred by a demonstrative element to something else. Originally the meaning was always an action; "is" of course meant "breathes." But now the verb has lost vitality by wear and tear, and only refers something to something else. The puzzle is that the Judgment is not referred to us who make it, but is expressed as if it was accomplished by something outside us. That puzzle points to the essential eature which we insisted on, viz. its objectivity; in predication we refer what is mentally our act to a subject that represents the real world, not to ourselves at all. When I say "Gladstone comes to London this week," the verb which expresses Gladstone's action also expresses that my real world in his person accepts the qualification "coming to London this week." Because of this objectivity of thought, I attribute to the real world and not to myself the connection which is presented to my mind, and so it takes its place as an act of the real world. But I might throw the whole content into the Predicate by saying, "The ideal content 'Gladstone coming to London this week' is a predication true of Reality." Thus though the distinction between Subject and Predicate best exhibits the living structure of knowledge, we must beware of the notion that two ideas or two things are needed for Judgment.

LECTURE VII [1]

THE CATEGORICAL AND HYPOTHETICAL CHARACTERS IN JUDGMENT

Some criticism on the ordinary scheme.

1. WE will first consider why we want to examine the types of Judgment, and then what arrangement of them best fulfils our want.

Why we need an arrangement.

(a) If we attended purely to the propositions in common use, we should get an unmanageable variety of forms, though the reality of thought would be fairly represented. We cannot quite do this ; we must try to select the forms which for some reason are the most fundamental and constant.

On the other hand, it is possible to think simply of what is convenient in logical combination ; and then for working with syllogistic Logic we get the well-known scheme of four propositions, each with Subject and Predicate ; and for working with symbolic Logic we get the existential scheme in which Subject and Predicate disappear, and " All S. are P." turns into " There exists no S. which is not P." ; or we get Jevons' Equational Logic, in which " All A is B " stands as $A = AB$. Now every Judgment has a great many aspects,

[1] Read Mill, ch. iv. (Bk. I.), on Propositions; Venn, *Empirical Logic*, ch. ix., x. Cf. *Knowledge and Reality*, pp. 57-8 ; and Venn, p. 264. Ordinary statement, Jevons, p. 60, ff. ; cf. p. 163.

being really a very complex systematic act of mind, and a logical method can be founded on any of these aspects which is sufficiently constant to stand for the Judgment. You can take " All men are mortal " to mean " There are no not-mortal men," or " Men = some mortals," or two or three more meanings. The two former are artificial or formal corollaries from the natural Judgment, representing it for some purposes but omitting a great part of its natural meaning. They tell you nothing about a relation of causality between the content of man and the property mortal, and they destroy all implication of existence in the Subject man.

What we want is neither to follow *mere* everyday language, nor be guided by mere convenience of logical combination. We want to look at the Judgment on its merits with reference to its power of expressing the principal kinds of our experience, which in fact are constructed in the medium of Judgment. The great kingdoms of intellectual experience are Perception, History, and Science, and of these three, Science, including Philosophy, is the form towards which all knowledge presses on, and its judgment must therefore be considered as the most complete type.

(β) With this purpose in mind, let us look at the traditional scheme, omitting the negative Judgments of which we have not yet spoken. We may dismiss the Indefinite Judgment " Men are mortal " as imperfect by not being " quantified," and we have left, as Categorical Judgments, the Particular Affirmative " Some men are mortal," the Universal Affirmative " All men are mortal," and the Singular Affirmative " Socrates is mortal." The Singular Affirmative, however, is not treated of any further under the old scheme, The common scheme.

I

because in it the Subject is taken in its full extent, and therefore the Singular Affirmative Judgment is ranked with the Universal Affirmative. So as Categorical Judgments we have left the Particular Affirmative and the Universal Affirmative.

Outside the account of the Categorical Judgment we find the Hypothetical and Disjunctive Judgments touched on as a sort of Appendix, standing as "Conditional." The historical reason of this is, that they were not recognised by Aristotle, and have never been incorporated in the diagram of judgments employed in traditional Logic. Then on the ordinary scheme we have—

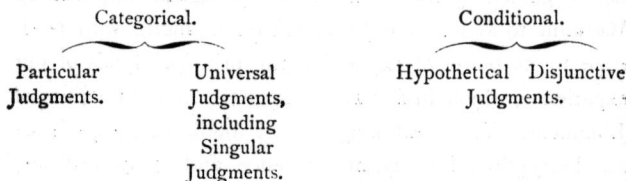

Categorical.		Conditional.	
Particular Judgments.	Universal Judgments, including Singular Judgments.	Hypothetical Judgments.	Disjunctive Judgments.

The defects of this scheme from our point of view are—

(i.) Our Impersonal and Demonstrative Judgments are omitted. They *might* be classed under the particular, which also has an undefined element in the subject.

(ii.) The Singular Judgment (of which the chief instance is the judgment with proper name) is rightly classed as Universal, but yet is wrongly absorbed in the abstract universal, from which it ought to be distinguished.

(iii.) In the treatment of the Universal Judgment there are two defects—

(1) The Collective Judgment, resulting from enumeration,

direct or indirect, is not distinguished from the Generic Judgment, resting on a connection of content or presumption of causality. "All the[1] papers have been looked over" should be distinguished from "All triangles have their three angles equal to two right angles."

(2) The nature of the Universal Judgment is not examined with a view to the distinction between Categorical and Hypothetical. The common Logic does not go behind the grammatical form, which on this point is not decisive.

(iv.) The Hypothetical Judgment[2] is said to consist of two categorical propositions, or to be "*complex*." But of course it is a simple judgment, *prima facie* expressing a relation of reason and consequent. Its parts are not Judgments, for they are not such as to stand alone.

(v.) The Disjunctive Judgment is often (*e. g.* by Mill and Bain) said to be equivalent to two Hypothetical Judgments. The strange thing is that both of these writers take the wrong two.[3] If we allow conversion of a Hypothetical Judgment two are enough, but of course they must be the two which cannot be got from each other by conversion, viz. the two beginning, "If A is B——" and "If A is not B——" respect-ively. If we do not admit conversion we must have all four. Let the disjunction be, "This signal light is either red or green." In order to know this we must know not

---

[1] "The" as here used indeed practically = "these," so that, by our analysis, such a judgment has no claim to rank as a universal judgment. It is difficult to find a plainly collective judgment which has not some affinity to judgment with demonstrative pronoun or proper name. A judgment in which "All M.P.'s" stands as subject, has affinity with the latter.

[2] Bain, p. 85 ; Jevons, p. 160.

[3] Mill, ch. iv. ; Bain, p. 86.

only that, "If it is red it is not green" (with its equivalent, "If it is green it is not red"), but that, "If it is not red it is green" (with its equivalent, "If it is not green it is red"). The former by itself leaves open the possibility that it may be not red or green, but blue or yellow; the latter by itself the possibility that when it is red it may also at the same time be green. The former secures that the two terms exclude each other; the latter, that, taken together, they exclude all other predicates.

In any case, the disjunctive is more than any combination of Hypotheticals, and really tends to be Categorical, and ought not to be claimed as Conditional.

Which are Categorical? 2. We will now look at these Judgments in order, consider their real meaning, and also ascertain the limits of the Categorical Judgment, viz. that which affirms the existence of its Subject, or in other words, asserts a fact.

The Particular Judgment. (1) The Particular Judgment of common Logic, "Some S. is P.," has different meanings according as it is understood naturally, or tied down to be a result of enumeration.

In any case it is an imperfect, unscientific Judgment, in which the mind cannot rest, because it has an undefined limitation imposed upon the Subject.

Its natural meaning. (a) For the natural meaning, take the example, "Some engines can drag a train at a mile a minute for a long distance."[1] This does not *mean* a certain number of engines, though of course they *are* a certain number. It

---

[1] To be accurate, the Judgment would demand the insertion of precise details about train, distance, and other matters. But this illustrates the point of the text, because the assignment of such details would naturally extend to the Subject, and then the "Some" would be displaced.

means certain engines of a particular make, not specified in the Judgment. The Judgment is Categorical, because the undefined reservation implies a reference to something unanalysed, but merely touched or presented in experience. If it was a mere idea it would have to be clear; and if the full description or definition were inserted, the Judgment would cease to affirm the existence of the engines in question. *And the Judgment itself challenges this completion.*

(β) A more artificial meaning is to take the Judgment A narrower meaning. as not formed by imperfect description, but by imperfect enumeration (understanding it almost wholly in denotation). "Some Conservatives are in favour of women's suffrage." This means or may mean that we have counted a certain number, large or small, who are so, and we may or may not know about the others. *Thus understood, the Judgment challenges complete enumeration;* it contains of course the elements of a fraction — half, most, nine-tenths of, and so on.

This again is Categorical; not merely because it implies counting, but because it implies counting units separately given to experience.

The Particular Judgment does not include our Impersonal and Demonstrative Judgments; they are not classed in the common text-books. But as referring to perception they too are categorical and assert facts, whether they have ideas to help out the perceptive reference or not. And there is no reason against including them under the Particular Judgment. The assertion, "This engine can drag a train a mile a minute," is much the same kind of Judgment as, "Some engines can, etc." Either of these would be false if no such engines existed. *These Judgments are of the essence of perception.* They have the connection of content and the undefined complex of presentation struggling together in them. They assert fact.

Singular Judgment. (2) The Singular Judgment of the common Logic is pretty much our Judgment with a proper name, which I call Individual, and which, as we saw, is in part rightly called universal—because the Subject extends beyond perception, and the Predicate follows the Subject. But it is a concrete or individual Universal, not an abstract Universal, and therefore asserts the existence of its Subject. The reason why it is taken to assert the reality of its Subject must be, I suppose, that it *can* assert this, its Subject being a name for an existence that has limited reality within the temporal series, and *cannot* assert anything else, not having any general fixed content or connotation which could imply a *general* connection of Subject and Predicate. The general connection of content which is so fatal to the asserting of fact does not exist in this case. We see this in Mill's instance. "The summit of Chimborazo is white." When the Subject is a unique name with precise connotation, "The centre of gravity of the material universe is variable," then we are passing into the abstract Universal, and I think we may take such a Judgment perhaps as one of the best examples of a conjunction of categorical and hypothetical meaning, *i. e.* of a connection of content ascribed to a Subject affirmed to exist. But usually one meaning or the other is uppermost.

These Judgments, called Singular or Individual, correspond to the region of history or narrative. The realities

with which they deal have their definite position in a single
system of time and space, and this is often made emphatic
by the use of tenses. But these change with the date
relative to the speaker, so that a Judgment with real tense
must once have been false, or must become false by
lapse of time. Thus the Judgment of fact may be not
absolutely true. Nothing is genuinely true which a change
of date can make false. The permanently true time-relations
between Subject and Predicate are determined by their
content, and the copula is not a tense, but a mere sign of
affirmation. The Singular as Categorical is sharply distinguished from the Abstract Universal, with which common
Logic classes it.

(3) Down to this point the judgment states a *fact*. When
we come to the ordinary universal affirmative, we see at once
that it may express very different meanings. In its natural
meaning it strongly *implies* that its Subject has a particular
existence within the series of time and space, but hardly
asserts it.

Universal Judgment.

Mill, for example, says "the objects are no longer individually designated, they are pointed out only by their attributes;"
" most of them not known individually at all." That means
that the explicit Subject is not made of individuals. The
natural meaning is disputed ; I incline to think with Venn,
that the Subject is naturally taken *more* in Denotation (not
solely, which is unmeaning), and the Predicate *more* in
connotation. But clearly in literal form the Subject is
simply a significant idea, and its existence in things or events
is not affirmed though it may be strongly implied. Hamilton [1]

Import of Proposi- tions.

---

[1] *Lectures*, vol. iii. p. 327.

says quite calmly—" 'Rainy weather is wet weather' is a Categorical Proposition; 'If it rains it will be wet' is Hypothetical." Between the two I can see no distinction of meaning at all.[1]   If indeed we take the Universal Affirmative in the pure sense of aggregate formed by enumeration, and therefore finite, it *may* be said that we assert the existence of the individuals composing it; but this is a very unreal view of the meaning of the Judgment (though suggested by its customary form), and even then it would be hard to prove that we continue to think of the Subject as individuals.   This reference to a finite aggregate makes the *Collective Judgment* or *Judgment of Allness*.   It cannot really exist in the case of a class like man, of unknown extension, and is confined, at its widest, to such cases as "All present Members of Parliament have to take a line on the Irish question."   This *might* be Categorical, but need not be so.

Otherwise, the Universal Affirmative of common Logic is literally Hypothetical, though in some cases it may strongly imply the assertion of reality.   Dr. Venn has discussed this question.[2]   He says the implication of existence is much stronger with a single-word Subject than with a many-worded Subject; *i. e.* perhaps with a natural than with an artificial conception.   But in any case, the expressed bond with perception is lost, and in pure form the Subject is a mere abstract idea, so that the relations of content entirely predominate over the implication of existence.

Thus the Universal Affirmative in its full meaning fairly

---

[1] Contrast Jevons, *Elementary Logic*, p. 163.
[2] *Empirical Logic*, pp. 258-9.

represents the sciences of classification, combining a sub-
ordinate meaning of Allness or numerical totality with a
primary meaning of connotation of attributes or presumed
causality. When we say "All the Buttercup family have an
inferior corolla," of course we mean that there is a reason for
this. Often we omit the term all, as in "Heat is a mode of
motion." In doing this we wipe out the last trace of a reference
to individual objects, and we pass to the pure hypothetical
form which absolutely neglects the existence of objects.

(4) The simplest type of this Judgment is, if A is B it "Hypo-
is C. This Judgment corresponds to abstract science, but thetical"
it is only making explicit what was implied in the Universal Judgment.
Affirmative. That expressed a presumption of causality,
this expresses a clear Reason and Consequent or scientific
necessity. The point of this form is (i.) that it drops all
reference to individual objects, (ii.) that it challenges you to
explain *how* the Subject-content is tied to the Predicate-
content. "Water boils at 212°," is a statement we should
generally pass in so-called Categorical form, because it does
not challenge any great accuracy of connection. But "If
water boils, it is at a temperature of 212°," puts us upon
asking, "Is the condition adequate?" and we see at once
that we must at least say, "If water boils *under pressure of
one atmosphere*, it is at a temperature of 212°," or else the
judgment is untrue. Of course we may apply the form
rightly or wrongly, as you may fill up your census paper
rightly or wrongly. We can only say that it calls upon you
to put in an adequate condition. Therefore I rather object
to the form "If A is, B is," because it adds very little to
the so-called Categorical shape.

We have now to ask how the Hypothetical Judgment connects its content with reality, *i. e.* how it is a Judgment at all? And the same explanation must apply to so-called Categorical Judgments, which can be thrown into this form without change of meaning.

The point from which the explanation starts is taking hypothesis as supposition. This is much more true, I think, than connecting it with *doubt*. In Dr. Venn's *Empirical Logic* the connection of Hypothetical Judgment and doubt to my mind disfigures the whole treatment of the Scientific Judgment. Supposition is distinct from affirmation—that is true—but just because it is distinct from affirmation, it cannot indicate doubt. It probably arose out of doubt, but as a method of science it does not imply doubt, but only the accurate limitation of attention. What doubt is there when we judge " If equals be added to equals, the wholes are equal "? We are attending to one particular thread of the nexus.

Hypothetical Judgment, then, is Judgment that starts from a supposition. Every supposition is made upon a certain basis of Reality. Take as an extreme case, " If you ask permission of A. B., he will refuse it." This is a supposition and its result, on the basis of the known character of A. B. And the full judgment is " A. B. is of such a character, that, supposing you ask him for permission, etc." The Hypothetical Judgment may be true, as an assertion about A. B.'s character, though you may never ask.

Here, then, is the clue to the analysis of *all Abstract Judgments*. Like Perceptive Judgment, they affirm something of Reality, but they do this indirectly and not directly

Underlying them there is the implied Categorical Judgment, " Reality has a character, such that, supposing so and so, the consequence will be so and so." And if this implied assertion is true, then the Hypothetical Judgment is true, although its terms may be not only unreal, but impossible. "If a microscopic object-lens with a focal length of $\frac{1}{100}$ in. were used, its magnifying power with an A eye-piece would be so many diameters." This is a mere matter of calcula-tion, and is unquestionably true, depending upon the effects of refraction upon the optical image. But I do not suppose that such an object-lens could be made, or used. Does such a Judgment, although true, express a *fact*? No, I should say not, although common usage varies. I remember a *Pall Mall* leading article which said, " It is an absolute fact, that, if Mr. Gladstone had not done something—the Government would have committed—some iniquity or other." Is this what we call a fact? We observe that the content actually mentioned was never real at all. The implied connection with reality is " There existed in reality a condi-tion of things (unspecified) in which *if* Mr. Gladstone, etc., etc." Are mathematical truths facts, and in what sense? Abstract truth need not, and perhaps cannot express fact, but implies fact indirectly.

(5) The Disjunctive Judgment "A is either B or C," is again not a judgment of doubt but a mode of Knowledge. It may be taken as numerical; then it gives rise to the statement of Chances. But in its perfect form it is appro-priate to the exposition of a content as a system, and it may be taken as returning to the Categorical Judgment, and combining it with the Hypothetical, because its

Disjunct-ive Judg-ment.

content is naturally taken as an individual, being necessarily concrete.

The peculiar point of the Disjunctive is that it makes negation positively significant.

"This signal light shows either red or green." Here we have the categorical element, "This signal light shows some colour," and on the top of this the two Hypothetical Judgments, "If it shows red it does not show green," "If it does not show red it does show green." You cannot make it up out of the two Hypothetical Judgments alone; they do not give you the assertion that "it shows some colour."[1]

Does this state a fact? I think it implies a fact much more distinctly than the hypothetical does, but of course it is a question whether an alternative can be called a fact. It seems a precise expression of some kinds of reality, but it is not a solid single momentary fact. It is very appropriate to the objects of philosophy as the higher concrete science, which are conceived as systems of facts bearing definite relations to each other; *e. g.* "Society is a structure of individual characters, having positions which are not interchangeable." Taken all as a mass, they are conjunctively connected, but taken in distinguishable relations they are disjunctively related. A human being as such has some position and no other, and this is ultimately determined by

[1] The example in the text, chosen for its simplicity, may be objected to as involving perceptive concreteness by the pronoun "this." You can have a disjunction, it may be said, dealing with "the triangle" as such; and why should this be more "Categorical" than the assertion that the triangle has its angles = three right angles? Still, it might be replied, the development of a single nature into a number of precise and necessary alternatives, always gives it an implication of self-completeness.

the nature of the social whole to which he belongs. He is if this, nothing else, and if nothing else, then this. A more artificial example, which illustrates the degree in which actual abstract knowledge and purpose can be embodied by man in machinery, is the interlocking system of points and signals at a great railway station. I suppose that the essence of such a system lies in arrangements for necessarily closing every track to all but one at a time of any tracks which cross it or converge into it. The track X receives trains from A, B, C, D; if the entrance for those from A is open, B, C, and D are *ipso facto* closed; if A, B, and C are closed, D is open, and so on. This is a disjunction consciously and purposely incorporated in material fact, and differs from a Disjunctive Judgment only in so far as existence necessarily differs from discursive thought.

The disjunction seems to complete the system of judgments, including all the others in itself, and it is wrong in principle to distinguish, *e. g.* between a hypothetical and categorical disjunction, or to consider how a disjunction can be denied. For disjunction in itself implies a kind of individuality which is beyond mere fact and mere abstract truth, though allied to both; and all intelligible negation is under, not of, a disjunction. Negation of a disjunction would mean throwing aside the whole of some definite group of thoughts as fallacious, and going back to begin again with a judgment of the simplest kind. It amounts to saying, " None of your distinctions touch the point; you must begin afresh."

LECTURE VIII[1]

NEGATION, AND OPPOSITION OF JUDGMENTS

Distinc-
tion be-
tween
Contrary
and Con-
tradictory
opposition.
1. THE only important point in the traditional diagram of the opposition of Judgments is the distinction between contrary and contradictory opposition, the opposition, that is, between A and E, and the opposition between A and O, or E and I.

In *Contrary* Opposition the one Judgment not only denies the other, but goes on to deny or assert something more besides. The mere grammatical shape "No man is mortal" conceals this, but we easily see that it says more than is necessary to deny the other, "All men are mortal."

In *Contradictory* Opposition, the one Judgment does absolutely nothing more than is involved in destroying the other.

The *Contrary* Negation has the advantage in positive, or at least in definite import.

The *Contradictory* or pure Negation has the advantage in the exhaustive disjunction which it involves.

This is plain if we reflect that Contrary Negation only

[1] Read Bain, pp. 55-6, on "Negative Names and the Universe of the Proposition," also on "Negative Propositions," p. 83 ff. ; Venn, *Empirical Logic*, pp. 214—217; Jevons, *Elementary Logic*, ix., on "Opposition of Propositions"; Mill, ch. iv. § 2.

rests on the Law of Contradiction, "X is not both A and not A."

Ordinary Diagram of Opposition of Judgments.

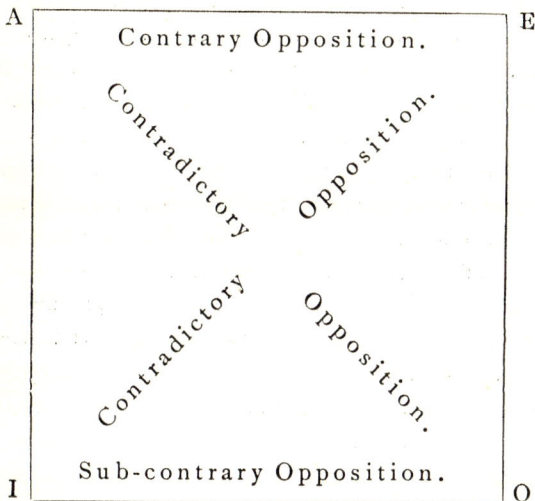

A

Contrary Opposition.

Contradictory

Opposition

Contradictory

Opposition.

Sub-contrary Opposition.

E

I

O

A = Universal Affirmative.   All men are mortal.
E = Universal Negative.   No men are mortal.
I = Particular Affirmative.   Some men are mortal.
O = Particular Negative.   Some men are not mortal.

Sub-contrary Opposition has no real meaning; the judgments so opposed are compatible.

It is not *true* both that "All M.P.'s are wise," *and* that "No M.P.'s are wise," but both may be false; while Contradictory Negation implies the Law of Excluded Third or excluded Middle, "X is either A or not A," the principle of disjunction, or rather, the simplest case of it. It is not *false* both that " All M.P.'s are wise " and that " Some M.P.'s are not wise." The point is, then, on the one hand, that in Contradiction you can go from falsehood to truth,[1] while in Contrariety you can only go from truth to falsehood ; but also that in Contradiction the Affirmative and Negative are not at all on a level in meaning, while in Contrariety they are much more nearly so. Then if we leave out the relations of mere plurality, of All and Some, which enable you to get contrary negation in pure negative form in the common Logic, we may say generally that in contrary negation something is asserted, and in contradictory negation taken quite literally nothing is asserted, but we have a "bare denial," a predicate is merely removed. In actual thought this cannot be quite realised, because a bare denial is really meaningless, and we always have in our mind some subject or universe of discourse within which the denial is construed definitely. But this definite construing is not justified by the bare form of contradiction, which consists simply in destroying a predication and not replacing it by another. In as far as you replace it by another, defined or undefined, you are going forward towards contrary negation.

Contrary Negation.

2. Thus, Contrary Negation in its essence is affirmation with a negative intention, and we may take as a type of it in this wider sense the affirmation of a positive character with the intention of denying another positive character. *E. g.* when you deny "This is a right-angled triangle" by asserting "This is an equilateral triangle," you have typical contrary negation. It is not really safe to speak of contraries except with reference to *judgments*, intended to deny each

---

[1] *I. e.* Contradictory alternatives are exhaustive.

other; but it is common to speak of species of the same genus as contraries or opposites, because the same thing cannot be both.[1]

We must therefore distinguish *contrary* from *different*. Of course the same thing or content has many different qualities, and even combines qualities that we are apt to call contrary or opposite. But as Plato was fond of pointing out, a thing cannot have different or opposing qualities in the same relation, that is to say, belonging to the same subject under the same condition. The same thing may be blue in one part of it and green in another, and the same part of it may be blue by daylight and green by candlelight. But the same surface cannot be blue and green at once by the same light to the same eye looking in the same direction. *Different* qualities become *contrary* when they claim to stand in the same relation to the same subject. Right-angled triangles and equilateral triangles do not deny each other if we leave them in peace side by side. They are then merely different species of the same genus, or different combinations of the same angular space. But if you say, " This triangle is right-angled," and I say " It is equilateral," then they deny each other, and become true contraries.

Then the *meaning* of denial is always of the nature of *contrary* denial. As we always speak and think within a general subject or universe of discourse, it follows that every denial substitutes some affirmation for the judgment which it denies. The only judgments in which this is not the case are those called by an unmeaning tradition Infinite Judgments, *i. e.* judgments in which the negative predicate

---

[1] Bain, p. 55 ff.

K

includes every determination which has applicability to the Subject. This is because the attribute denied has no applicability to the Subject, and therefore all that has applicability is undiscriminatingly affirmed, in other words, the judgment has no meaning. "Virtue is not-square." This suggests no definite positive quality applicable to virtue, and therefore is idle. You may safely analyse a significant negative judgment, "A is not B" as = "A is not B but C," or as = "A is X, which excludes B." For X may be undetermined, "a colour not red." But then if the meaning is always affirmative or positive, why do we ever use the negative form?

Why use Negation? 3. In the first place, we use it because it indicates exclusion, and without it we cannot distinguish between mere differents on the one hand and contraries on the other. If you ask me, "Are you going to Victoria, London Chatham and Dover station?" and I answer, "I am going to Victoria, London Brighton and South Coast," that will not be satisfactory to you, unless you happen to know beforehand that these stations are so arranged that if you are at one you are not at the other. They might be a single station used by different companies, and called indifferently by the name of either. To make it clear that the suggestion and the answer are incompatible, I must say, "I am *not* going to Victoria, London Chatham and Dover," and I may add or not add, "I *am* going to Victoria, London Brighton and South Coast." That tells you that the one predicate excludes the other, and that is the first reason why we use the generalised form of exclusion, *i. e.* negation.

But in the second place, it can give us more, and something absolutely necessary to our knowledge, and that is not merely exclusion, but exhaustion. In literal form negation is absolutely exhaustive, that is to say, contradictory. The Judgment "A is not B" forms an exhaustive alternative to the Judgment "A is B," so that no third case beyond these two is possible, and therefore you can argue from the false-hood of either to the truth of the other. Now this form is potentially of immense value for knowledge, and all disjunc-tion consists in applying it; but as it stands in the abstract it is worthless, because it is an empty form. "A is red or not-red." If either of these is false the other is true. But what do you gain by this? You are not entitled to put any positive meaning upon not-red; if you do so you slide into mere contrary negation, and the inference from falsehood becomes a fallacy. Make an argument, "The soul is red or not-red." "It is not-red ∴ it is some other colour than red." The argument is futile. We have con-strued "not-red" as a positive contrary, and that being so, the disjunction is no longer exhaustive. We had no right to say that the soul is either red or some other colour; the law of Excluded Middle does not warrant that.

I pause to say that the proof of the exhaustiveness of negation, *i. e.* that two negatives make an affirmative—that if A is not not-B, it follows that A is B—is a disputed problem, the problem known as double negation. How do you know that what is not not-red must be red? I take the law of Excluded Middle simply as a definition of the bare form of denial, or the distinction between this and not-this; "not-this" being the bare abstraction of the other than this. Others say that every negation presupposes an affirmation; so "A is not-B" presupposes the affirmation "A is B," and if you knock down the negative, the original affirmative is left standing. Sigwart and B. Erdmann say this. I think it monstrous. I do not believe that you must find an affirmative standing before you can deny.

Stage of Significant Negation. Combination of Contrary and Contradictory.

4. Well, then, the point we have reached is this. What we mean in denial is always the contrary, something positive. What we say in denial—in other words, the literal form which we use—always approaches the contradictory, *i. e.* is pure exclusion. The Contrary of the diagram denies more than it need, but still its form is that of exclusion. Now we have seen that in denial, as used in common speech, we get the benefit of *both affirmation and exclusion,* but in accurate thought we want to do much more than this; we want to get the whole benefit of the negative form—that is, to get a positive meaning together with not only exclusion, but exhaustion.

I will put the three cases in one example, beginning with mere affirmations of different facts.

Different Affirmations.

(1) "He goes by this train to-day." "He goes by that train to-morrow." This conjunction, as simply stated, gives *no* inference from the truth or falsehood of either statement to the truth or falsehood of the other.

Contrary Opposition, exclusive.

(2) "He goes by this train," and "He goes by that train," with a meaning equivalent to "No, he goes by that." If it is true that in the sense suggested by the context he goes by this train, then it is not true that he goes by the other, and if it is true, in the sense explained, that he goes by the other, then he does not go by this. Each excludes the other, but both may be excluded by a third alternative. If it is *not* true that he goes by this train—

nothing follows. There may be any number of trains he might go by, or he might give up going; *i. e.* your Universe of discourse, your implicit meaning is not expressly limited. If it is *not* true to say, "No, he goes by that"—taking the whole meaning together, and not separating its parts, for this combination is essential to the "contrary"—nothing follows as to the truth of the other statement. He may not be going at all, or may be going by some third train, or by road.

But if you limit your Universe, or general subject, then you can combine the value of contrary and contradictory negation. Then you say,

(3) "He goes either by this train or by that." Then you can infer not only from "He goes by this train," that "He does not go by that," but from "He does not go by this train" to "He does go by that." Combined Contrary and Contradictory Negation.

The alternative between "A is B" and "A is not-B" remains exhaustive, but not-B has been given a positive value, *because we have limited the possibilities by definite knowledge.* The processes of accurate thinking and observation aim almost entirely at giving a positive value C to not-B, and a positive value B to not-C, under a disjunction, because it is then that you define exactly where and within what conditions C which is not B passes into B which is not C. Take the disjunction, "Sound is either musical or noise." If the successive vibrations are of a uniform period it is musical sound; if they are of irregular periods it is noise. This is a disjunction which assumes the form,

A is either B or C. That is to say, If it is B it is not C. If it is not B it is C.

Therefore I think that all "determination is negation "—of course, however, not bare negation, but significant negation ; the essence of it consists in correcting and confirming our judgment of the nature of a positive phenomenon by showing that *just when* its condition ceases, *just then* something else begins, and when you have exhausted the whole operation of the system of conditions in question, so that from any one phase of their effects you can read off what *it* is not but the *others* are, then you have almost all the knowledge we can get. The "*Just-not*" is the important point, and this is only given by a positive negation within a definite system. You want to explain or define the case in which A becomes B. You want observation of not-B ; but almost the whole world is formally or barely not-B, so that you are lost in chaos. What you must do is to find the point within A, where A_1 which is B passes into A_2 which is C, and that will give you the *just-not*-B which is the valuable negative instance.

Negative Judgment expressing fact. 5. You will find it said that a Negative Judgment cannot express fact ; *e. g.* that a Judgment of Perception cannot be negative. This is worth reflecting upon ; I hope that what has been said makes clear how far it is true. The bare form of Negation is not adequate to fact ; it contains mere emptiness or ignorance ; we nowhere in our perception come upon a mere "not-something." No doubt negation is in this way more subjective than affirmation. But then as it fills up in meaning, the denial becomes more and more on a level with the affirmation, till at last in systematic knowledge both become double-edged—every affirmative denies, and every negative affirms. When a man who is both a musician and a physicist says, "this compound tone A is a discord Y," he knows exactly how much of a discord, what ratio of vibration makes it so much of a discord, how much it would have to change to become a concord (X which is not Y), and what change in the vibration ratio from a_1 to a_2 would be needed to make it a concord. To such knowledge as this, the accurate negation is just as expressive as the affirmation, and it does not matter whether he says "A is Y," or "A is by so much not X." It becomes, as Venn says, all but impossible to distinguish the affirmation from the negation. No doubt affirmative terms come in at this stage, though the meaning is negative. Observe in this connection how we sometimes use the nearest word we can think of, knowing that the negative gives the positive indirectly—"He was, I won't say insolent," meaning *just not* or "*all but*" insolent ; or again, "That was not right," rather than saying bluntly "wrong."

6. Every significant negation "A is not B " can be analysed as "A is X which excludes B." Of course X may not be a distinct C ; *e. g.* we may be able to see that A is not red, but we may not be able to make out for certain what colour it is ; then the colour X is "an unknown colour which excludes red." ^{Operation of the denied idea.}

How does the rejected idea operate in Judgment ? I suppose it operates by suggesting a Judgment which as you make it destroys some of its own characteristics. It is really an expression of the confirmatory negative instance or "just-not." *Just* when two parallel straight lines swing so that they can meet, *just* then the two interior angles begin to be less than two right angles, which tells us that the straight lines are ceasing to be parallel. Just in as much as two straight lines begin to enclose a space we become aware that one or other of them is not straight, so that A in turning from Y to X turns *pari passu* from A_1 to A_2, and we are therefore justified in saying that A, when it is Y, cannot be X.

This lecture may pave the way for Induction, by giving some idea of the importance of the negative instance which Bacon preached so assiduously.

In a real system of science the conceptions are negative towards each other merely as defining each other. One of them is not in itself more negative than another. Such a conception, *e. g.*, is that of a triangle compared with two parallel straight lines which are cut by a third line. If the parallels are swung so as to meet, they become a triangle which gains in its third angle what the parallels lose on the two interior angles, and the total of two right angles remains the same. Thus in saying that parallels cut by a third straight line cannot form a triangle, and that the three angles of a triangle are equal to two right angles, we are expressing the frontier which is at once the demarcation between two sets of geometrical relations, and the positive grasp or connection of the one with the other. The negation is no bar to a positive continuity in the organism of the science, but is essential to defining its nature and constituent elements. This is the bearing of significant negation when fully developed.

INFERENCE AND THE SYLLOGISTIC FORMS

1. THE Problem of Inference is something of a paradox. Inference consists in asserting as fact or truth, on the ground of certain given facts or truths, something which is not included in those data. We have not got inference unless the conclusion, (i.) is necessary from the premisses, and (ii.) goes beyond the premisses. To put the paradox quite roughly—we have not got inference unless the conclusion is (i.) in the premisses, and (ii.) outside the premisses. This is the problem which exercises Mill so much in the chapter, "Function and Value of the Syllogism." We should notice especially his § 7, "the universal type of the reasoning process." The point of it is to make the justice of inference depend upon relations of content, which are judged of by what he calls induction. That is quite right, but the question still returns upon us, "What kind of relations of content must we have, in order to realise the paradox of Inference?" This the "type of inference" rather shirks. See Mill's remarks when he is brought face to face with

Inference in general.

[1] Read for Lectures IX. and X., Mill, Bk. II. ch. i., ii., iii. ; Bk. III. ch. i. and ii. at least ; Venn, ch. xiv., xv. ; Jevons, *Lessons,* xv. and xxiv. ; De Morgan's *Budget of Paradoxes.*

Induction, Bk. III. ch. i. § 2. An Inference, as he there recognises, either does not hold at all, or it holds "in all cases of a certain description," *i. e.* it depends on universals.

I ought to warn you at once that though we may have novelty in the conclusion of Inference (as in multiplication of large numbers), the necessity is more essential than the novelty. In fact, much of Inference consists in demonstrating the *connection* of matters that as *facts* are pretty familiar. Of course, however, they are always modified in the process, and in that sense there is always novelty. You obtain the most vital idea of Inference by starting from the conclusion as a suggestion, or even as an observation, and asking yourself how it is proved, or explained, and treating the whole process as a single mediate judgment, *i. e.* a reasoned affirmation. Take the observation, "The tide at new and full moon is exceptionally high." In scientific inference this is filled out by a middle term. We may profitably think of the " middle term," as the copula or grip which holds the conclusion together, made explicit and definitely stated. Thus the judgment pulls out like a telescope, exhibiting fresh parts within it, as it passes into inference. "The tide at new and full moon, *being at these times the lunar tide plus the solar tide*, is exceptionally high." This is the sort of inference which is really commonest in science. Such an inference *would* no doubt give us the conclusion if we did not know it by observation, but it happens in many cases that we do know it by observation, and what the inference gives us is the connection, which of course may enable us to correct the observation.

2. In the strictest formal sense there can be no inference *Conditions* from particulars to particulars. When there seems to be *of the possibility of such inference*, it is merely that the ground of inference *Inference.* is not mentioned, sometimes because it is obvious, sometimes because it is not clearly specified in the mind. Suppose we say, " Morley and Harcourt will go for Disestablishment, and I think, therefore, that Gladstone will." I do not *express* any connecting link, merely because every one sees at once that I am inferring from the intentions of some Liberal leaders to those of another. If the terms are really particulars, " X is A, Y is B, Z is C," one is helpless ; they do not point to anything further at all ; there is no bridge from one to the other.

Inference cannot possibly take place except through the medium of an identity or universal which acts as a bridge from one case or relation to another. If each particular was shut up within itself as in the letters taken as an instance just now, you could never get from one which is given to another which is not given, or to a connection not given between two which are given.

Take the simplest conceivable case, which hardly amounts to Inference, that of producing a given straight line. How is it that this is possible ? Because the direction of the straight line is universal and self-identical as against possible directions in space, and it acts as a rule which carries you beyond the given portion of it. This might fairly be called an "immediate inference." So I presume that any curve can be constructed out of a sufficient portion of the curve, although, except with a circle, this is more than repeating the same line over again. The content has a nature which is capable of prescribing its own continuation. A curve is not a direction; a truth which is a puzzle to the non-mathematician—it is a law of continuous change of direction.

System the ultimate condition of Inference.

3. *Ultimately* the condition of inference is always a system. And it will help us in getting a vital notion of inference if we think, to begin with, of the interdependence of relations in space—in geometrical figures, or, to take a commonplace example, in the adjustment of a Chinese puzzle or a dissected map. Or any of the propositions about the properties of triangles are a good example. How can one property or attribute determine another, so that you can say, " Given this, there must be that "? This can only be answered by pointing to the nature of a whole with parts, or a system, which just means this, a group of relations or properties or things so held together by a common nature that you can judge from some of them what the others must be. Not all systems admit of precise calculation and demonstration, but wherever there is inference at all there is at least an identity of content which may be more or less developed into a precise relation between parts. For example, we cannot construct geometrically the life and character of an individual man; we can argue from his character to some extent, but the connection of facts in his personal identity is all that we can infer for certain; and even this involves a certain context of facts, as in circumstantial evidence. Yet this simplest linking together of occurrences by personal identity is enough to give very startling inferences. Thackeray's story of the priest is a good instance of inference from mere identity. " An old abbé, talking among a party of intimate friends, happened

to say, ' A priest has strange experiences ; why, ladies, my first penitent was a murderer.' Upon this, the principal nobleman of the neighbourhood enters the room. ' Ah, Abbé, here you are ; do you know, ladies, I was the Abbé's first penitent, and I promise you my confession astonished him ! ' " Here the inference depends solely on individual identity, which is, as we saw, a kind of universal.

But in this case was there really an inference ? Does not the conclusion fall inside the premisses ? It must in one sense fall inside the premisses, or it is not true. But it does not fall inside them until we have brought them into contact by their point of identity and melted them down into the same judgment. I admit that these inferences from individual identity, assuming the terms not to be ambiguous, are only just within the line of rational inference, but, as we see in this case, they bring together the parts of a very extended universal. What *is* the lower limit of inference ?

4. In the doctrine of *immediate Inference* common Logic treats of Conversion and the Opposition of judgments.

Immediate Inference.

Is a mere transposition of Subject and Predicate, where the truth of the new judgment follows from that of the old, an inference ? It is a matter of degree.[1] Does it give anything new ? " The Queen is a woman." " A woman is the Queen." If we make a real difference between the implications of a Subject and a Predicate, we seem to get something new ; but it is a point of little interest. Com-

---

[1] The collective or general judgment, as commonly explained, cannot be converted "simply," because the predicate is "wider" than the subject, and the same rule is accepted for the relation of consequent to antecedent. The aim of science, it might almost be said, is to get beyond the kind of judgment to which this rule applies.

parison or Recognition are more like immediate inferences. Comparison means that we do not let ourselves perceive freely, but take a particular content as the means of apperception of another content, *i. e.* as the medium through which we look at it. I do not merely look at the second, but I look at it with the first in my mind. And so far I may be said to infer, without the form of proof, from data of perception to a relation between them. "You are taller than me," is a result obtained by considering your height from the point of view of mine, or *vice versa*. Recognition is somewhat similar. It is more than a mere perception, because it implies reproduction of elements not given, and an identification with them. I recognise this man *as* so-and-so, *i. e.* I see he is identical with the person who did so-and-so. It is a judgment, but it goes beyond the primary judgment, "He is such and such," and is really inferred from it. It is a matter of degree. Almost every Judgment can be broken up into elements, and recognition fades gradually into cognition—we "recognise" an example of a law, a right, a duty, an authority ; not that we knew *it*, the special case, before, but that in analysing it we find a principle which commands our assent, and with which we identify the particular instance before us.

Number of Instances.   5. The difference between guess-work and demonstration rests on the difference between a detached quality or relation striking enough to suggest something to us, and a system thoroughly known in its parts as depending on one another. This is so even in recognising an individual person ; it is necessary to know that the quality by which you recognise him is one that no one else possesses, or else it is guess-work. Still more is this the case in attempting a scientific connection. All scientific connection is really by system as between the parts of the content. A quality is often forced on our attention by being repeated a great many times in some particular kind of occurrence, but as long as we do not know its *causal* connection with the properties and relations involved in the occurrence it is only guess-work to treat them as essentially connected. This is a matter very easy to confuse, and very important. It is easy to confuse, because a number of instances does help us really in inference, as it always insensibly gives us an immense command of content; that is to say, without knowing it we correct and enlarge our idea of the probable connection a little with every instance. So the connection between the properties that strike us becomes much larger and also more correct than it is to people who have only seen a few instances. But this is because the instances are all a little different, and so correct each other, and show transitions from more obvious forms to less obvious forms of the properties in question which lead us up to a true understanding of them. If the instances were all exactly the same they would not help us in this way, but our guess would still be a guess, however many instances might have suggested it.

I remember that a great many years ago I hardly believed in the stone-age tools being really tools made by men. I had only seen a few bad specimens, one or two of which I still think were just accidentally broken flints which an old country clergyman took for stone-age tools. This was to me then a mere guess, viz. that the cutting shape proved the flints to have been made by men. And obviously, if I had seen hundreds of specimens no better than these, I should have treated it as a mere guess all the same. But I happened to go to Salisbury, and there I saw the famous Blackmore Museum, where there are not only hundreds of specimens, but specimens arranged in series from the most beautiful knives and arrow-heads to the rudest. There one's eye caught the common look of them at once, the better specimens helping one to interpret the worse, and the guess was almost turned into a demonstration, because one's eyes were opened to the sort of handwork which these things exhibit, and to the way in which they are chipped and flaked.

Now this very important operation of number of examples, in helping the mind to an explanation, is always being confused with the effect of mere repetition of examples, which does not help you to an explanation, *i. e.* a repetition in which one tells you no more than another. But these mere repetitions operate *prima facie* in a different way, viz. by making you think there is an *unknown* cause in favour of the combination of properties which recurs, and lead up to the old-fashioned perfect Induction and the doctrine of chances, and not to demonstration.[1]

On the road from guess-work to demonstration, and generally assisted by great experience, we have *skilful* guess-

---

[1] Ultimately the calculus of chances may be said to rest on the same principle as Induction, in so far as the repetition of examples derives its force from the (unspecified) variety of contexts through which this repetition shows a certain result to be persistent. But in such a calculus the presumption from recurrence in such a variety of contexts is only estimated, and not analysed.

work, the first stage of discovery. This depends on the
capacity for hitting upon qualities which *are* connected by
causation, though the connection remains to be proved. So
a countryman or a sailor gets to judge of the weather; it is
not merely that he has seen so many instances, but he has
been taught by a great variety of instances to recognise the
essential points, and has formed probably a much more
complex judgment than he can put into words. So again a
doctor or a nurse can see how ill a patient is, though it
does not follow that they could always say why this appearance goes with this degree of illness. In proportion as you
merely *presume* a causal connection, it is guess-work or pure
discovery. In as far as you can *analyse* a causal connection
it is demonstration or proof; and for Logic, discovery
cannot be treated apart from proof, except as skilful guess-
work. *In as far as* there is ground for the guess, so far it
approaches to proof; *in as far as* there is no ground, it
gives nothing for Logic to get hold of—is mere caprice. A
good scientific guess really depends on a shrewd eye for the
essential points. I am not mathematician enough to give
the history of the discovery of Neptune by Leverrier and
Adams, "calculating a planet into existence by enormous
heaps of algebra,"[1] but it must have begun as a guess. I
should suppose it was suggested before Adams and Leverrier
took it up, on the ground of the anomalous movements of
Uranus indicating an attraction unaccounted for by the
known solar system. And I suppose that this guess would
gradually grow into demonstration as it became clear that
nothing but a new planet would explain the anomalies of

[1] De Morgan, *Budget of Paradoxes*, p. 53.

L

the orbit of Uranus. And at last the calculators were able to tell the telescopist almost exactly where to look for the unknown planet. The proof in this case preceded the observation or discovery by perception, and this makes it a very dramatic example; but if the observation had come earlier, it would not I suppose have dispensed with the precise proof of Neptune's effect on Uranus. though it might have made it easier.

Figures of Syllogism. 6. In illustration of this progress from guess-work to science,[1] I will give an example of the three Aristotelian figures of the Syllogism. I omit the fourth. I assume that the heavier term, or the term most like a "thing," is fitted to be the Subject, and the term more like an attribute to be the Predicate. The syllogistic rules depend practically on the fact that common Logic, following common speech and thought, treats the Predicate as wider than the Subject, which corresponds to Mill's view (also the common scientific view), that the same effect may have several alternative causes (not a compound cause, but different possible causes), and that consequent is wider than antecedent.[2] It is this assumption that prevents affirmative propositions from being simply convertible, *i. e.* prevents "All men are mortal" from being identical with "All mortals are men," and but for it there would be no difference of figure at all, as there is not for inference by equation.

This progression is here merely meant to illustrate the universal or systematic connection of particulars in process of disengaging itself. But I do *not* say that the first

---

[1] Cf. Plato's *Republic*, Bk. VI., end.
[2] See p. 141, *note.*

figure with a major premise is a natural form for all arguments.

I take the scheme of the first three figures from Jevons. and suggest their meaning as follows :—

> X denotes the major term.
> Y   ,,   ,, middle term.
> Z   ,,   ,, minor term.

		1st Fig.		2nd Fig.		3rd Fig
Major Premise	...	Y X	...	X Y	...	Y X
Minor ,,	...	Z Y	...	Z Y	...	Y Z
Conclusion	...	Z X	...	Z X	...	Z X

Fig. 3. *An observation and a guess.*

Yesterday it rained in the evening.

All yesterday the smoke tended to sink.

∴ The smoke sinking $\left(\begin{matrix} \text{may be} \\ \text{is sometimes} \end{matrix}\right)$ a sign of rain.

The conclusion cannot be general in this figure, because nothing general has been said in the premisses about the subject of the conclusion. So it is very suitable for a mere suggested connection given in a single content—that of the time "yesterday," implying moreover that both the points in question have something to do with the state of the atmosphere on that single day.

Fig. 2. *A tentative justification.*

Smoke that goes downwards is heavier than air

Particles of moisture are heavier than air.

∴ Particles of moisture may be in the descending smoke.

A universal conclusion in this figure would be formally bad. But we do not care for that, because we only mean it to be tentative, and we do not draw a universal affirmative conclusion. We express its badness by querying it, or by saying "may be." The reason why it is formally bad is that nothing general has been said in the premises about the middle term or reason, so that it is possible that the two Subjects do not touch each other within it, *i. e.* that the suggested special cause, moisture, is not connected with the special effect, the sinking of the smoke. The general reason " heavier than air " may include both special suggested cause and special suggested effect without their touching. Smoke and moisture may both sink in air, but for different and unconnected reasons. Still, when a special cause is suggested which is probably present in part, and which would act in the way required by the general character of the effect, there is a certain probability that it *is* the operative cause, subject to further analysis ; and the argument has substantive value, though bad in form. The only good arguments in this figure have negative conclusions, *e. g.*—

Smoke that is heavier than air goes downwards.

Smoke on dry days does not go downwards.

∴ Smoke on dry days is not heavier than air.

This conclusion *is* formal, because the negative throws the second Subject altogether outside the Predicate, and so outside the first Subject. The one content always has a characteristic which can never attach to the other, and consequently it is clear that some genuine underlying difference keeps them apart. Such an inference would corroborate the suggestion previously obtained that the presence of moisture was the active cause of the descending smoke on days when rain was coming.

Fig. 1. *A completely reasoned judgment.*

All particles that sink in the air in damp weather more than in dry, are loaded with moisture when they sink.

Smoke that descends before rain is an example of particles that sink in the air in damp weather more than in dry.

∴. Smoke that descends before rain is loaded with moisture when it descends (and therefore its sinking is not accidentally a sign of rain, but is really connected with the cause of rain).

The major premise belongs only to this figure. In the other it is mere tradition to call it so, and their two premisses are the same in kind, and contribute equally to the conclusion, and for that reason the affirmative conclusion was not general or not formal. If your general conclusion is to follow by mere form, you must show your principle as explicitly covering your conclusion. But if you do this, then of course you are charged with begging the question. And, in a sense, that is what you mean to do, when you set out to make your argument complete by its mere form. If you have *bonâ fide* to construct a combination of your data, you cannot predict whether the conclusion will take this form or that form. Using a major premise meant, " We have got a principle that covers the conclusion, and so explains the case before us." Granting that the major premise involves the minor premise and conclusion, that is just the reason why it is imperative to express them. The meaning of the Syllogism is that it analyses the whole actual thought ; the fault is to suppose that novelty is the point of inference. The Syllogism shows you how you must understand either premise in order that it may cover the conclusion. Or, starting from the conclusion as a current popular belief, or as an isolated observation or suggestion by an individual observer (and this is practically the way in which our science on any subject as a rule takes its rise), the characteristic process through the three stages described above consists in first noting the given circumstances under which, according to the *prima facie* belief or observation, the conjunction in question takes place ("yesterday," *i. e.* "in the state of the atmosphere yesterday"); secondly in analysing or considering those given circumstances, to find within them something which looks like a general property, a law, or causal operation, which may attach the conjunction in question to the systematic whole of our experience (the presence of something heavier than air in the atmosphere); and thirdly, in the exhibition of this ground or reason as a principle, in the light of which the primary belief or observation (probably a good deal modified) becomes a part of our systematic intelligible world.

LECTURE X[1]

INDUCTION, DEDUCTION, AND CAUSATION

1. INDUCTION has always meant some process that starts Induction. from instances; the Greek word for it is used by Aristotle both in his own Logic and in describing the method of Socrates. It meant either "bringing up instance after instance," or "carrying the hearer on by instances." And still in speaking of Induction we think of some process that consists in doing something with a number of instances. But we find that this notion really breaks down, and the contradiction between Mill and other writers (Jevons, ch. i.) shows exactly how it breaks down. The question is whether one experiment will establish an inductive truth. We will review the meanings of the term, and show how they change.

(*a*) Induction by simple enumeration was what Bacon was Induction by simple Enumeration. always attacking, and saying, quite rightly, that it was not scientific. It is the method which I stated in the Third Figure of the syllogism, almost a conversational method; the mere beginning of observation. "I am sure the influenza is a serious illness; all my friends who have had it have been dreadfully pulled down."

[1] Read N. Lockyer's *Elements of Astronomy;* Abney's *Colour Measurement;* Introduction to *Bain on Induction;* Jevons's *Elementary Lessons on "Observation and Experiment,"* p. 228, and on *Induction,* p. 214 (about Mill).

A B C have been seriously ill.

A B C have had influenza.

∴ Influenza is a serious illness.

Now this popular kind of inference, as Bacon says, "Precarie concludit, et periculo exponitur ab instantia contradictoria." Suppose you come across one slight case of influenza, the conclusion is upset. This type of reasoning really appeals to two quite opposite principles; one the principle of counting, which leads up to statistics and the old-fashioned perfect Induction or the theory of chance, the other the principle of scientific system.

Enumeration always has a ground. (*b*) In counting, we do not think of the reason why we count, but there always is a reason, which is given in the nature of the whole whose parts we are counting. If I count the members of this audience, it is because I want to know how many units the whole audience consists of. I do not ask why each unit is there; counting is different from scientific analysis; but yet the connection between whole and part is present in *my reason for counting*. So really, though I only say, "One, two, three, four, etc.," each unit demands a judgment, "This is one member— that makes two members, that makes three members," etc. Counting is the construction of a total of units sharing a common nature; measurement is a form of counting in which the units are also referred to some other standard besides the whole in question, *e. g.* the standard pound or inch.

Perfect Induction. (*c*) *Mere* counting or "enumeration" only helps you in induction by comparison with some other numerical result, and, if imperfect, only to the extent of suggesting that there

is a common cause or there is not a common cause. *E.g.*
if you throw a six with one die fifty times running, you
infer that the die is probably loaded. This is because you
compare the result with that which you expect if the die
is fair, viz. a six once in every six throws. You infer that
there is a special cause favouring one side. The principle
is that ignorance is impartial. If you know no reason for
one case more than another, you take them as equal
fractions of reality; if results are not equal fractions of
reality, you infer a special reason favouring one case.[1] Pure
counting cannot help you in Induction in any way but this.
Perfect Induction simply means that the total is limited and
the limit is reached; you have counted 100 per cent. of
the possible cases, and the chance becomes certainty. The
result is a mere collective judgment.

(*d*) The principle of scientific system is quite a different System.
thing. Essentially, it has nothing to do with number or
with a generalised conclusion. It is merely this, "What is
once true is always true, and what is not true never was
true." The aim of scientific induction is to find out "What
is true," *i. e.* what is consistent with the given system. We
never doubt this principle; if we did we could have no
science. If observation contradicts our best-established
scientific laws, and we cannot suppose an error in the
observation, we must infer that the law was wrongly, *i. e.*
untruly stated. Therefore, as Mill says, one case is enough,
if you can find the truth about it. People object that you
cannot make a whole science out of one case, and therefore you must have a number of instances. That is a

[1] See Lecture IX., p. 144, *note.*

practical point to be borne in mind, but it has no real
scientific meaning. "Instance" cannot be defined except
as one observation, which is a purely accidental limitation.
The point is, that you use your instances not by counting
cases of given terms, but by ascertaining what the terms
really are (*i. e.* modifying them), and what is their real connection. This is the simple secret of Mill's struggle to base
scientific Induction, on Induction by simple Enumeration ;
the latter is not the evidence, but the beginning of eliciting
the evidence—so that the Scientific Induction is far more
certain than that on which Mill bases it. Aristotle's statement
is the clearest and profoundest that has ever been made.

Aristotle, *An. Post.* 87, b. 28.

"Nor is it possible to obtain scientific knowledge by way
of sense-perception. For even if sense-perception reveals a
certain character in its object, yet we necessarily perceive
this, *here*, and *now*. The universal, which is throughout all,
it is impossible to perceive ; for it is not a this-now ; if it
had been it would not have been universal, for what is
always and everywhere we call universal. Since then
demonstration (science) is universal, and such elements it
is impossible to perceive by sense, it is plain that we cannot
obtain scientific knowledge by way of sense. But it is clear
that even if we had been able to perceive by sense [*e. g.*
by measurement] that the three angles of a triangle are
equal to two right angles, we should still have had to search
for a demonstration, and should not, as some say, have
known it scientifically (without one) ; for we necessarily
perceive in particular cases only, but science comes by
knowing the universal. Wherefore if we could have been
on the moon, and seen the earth coming between it and the

sun, we should not (by that mere perception) have *known* the cause of the eclipse. Not but what by seeing this frequently happen we should have grasped the universal, and obtained a demonstration; for the universal becomes evident out of a plurality of particulars, and the universal is valuable because it reveals the cause;" and again,[1] "And that the search of science is for the middle term is made plain in those cases in which the middle term is percep tible to sense. For we search where we have had no per- ception,—as for the reason (or middle term) of an eclipse,— to know if there is a reason or not. But if we had been upon the moon, we should not have had to inquire if the process (of an eclipse as such, and not some other kind of darkness) takes place, or for what reason, but both would have been plain at once. The perception would have been, 'The earth is now coming between,' carrying with it the obvious fact, 'The moon is now suffering an eclipse,' and *out of this* the universal (connection) would have arisen."

(*e*) I showed you a method on the way to this in the shape Analogy of Aristotle's second figure, which we may call *analogy*. The plain sign of it is, that you give up counting the in- stances and begin to weigh them, so that the attributes which are predicates fall into the middle term or reason In the former inference about influenza we did not suppose that you had any idea *why* influenza was a serious illness; but in analogy there is some suggestion of this kind, so that the connection is examined into. Here at once you begin to get suggested explanations and confirmation from the

[1] Aristotle, *An. Post.*, 90, a 24.

system of knowledge. You cannot have analogy by merely counting attributes.

I begin from *Enumerative Suggestion* drawn from observation of Butterflies.

1. Three species of genus x closely resemble three species of y.

2. The species of x would be protected by resembling y (because y is distasteful to birds).

∴ The resemblance may be a "protective resemblance," *i. e.* a resemblance brought about by survival of those thus protected.

On this there naturally follows *Analogy*.

1. Protective resemblances naturally increase through series of species from slighter to closer resemblances.

2. The resemblances in question increase in genus x through series of species from slighter to closer resemblance to y.

∴ The resemblances in question show important signs of being protective resemblances.

When we get thus far, a single syllogism will not really represent the argument. It can only analyse with convenience a single step in inference. But now we have connected the reason of the resemblances with the whole doctrine of natural selection, the gradual approximation of the species is most striking, and we could set up a corroborative analogy on the basis of every feature and detail of these resemblances, the tendency of which would be to show that no cause or combination of causes other than that suggested is likely to account for the observed resemblances.

I give a confirmatory negative analogy.

1. No protective resemblance can grow up where there is no initial tendency to resemblance.

2. The non-resembling species in the genus x show no initial tendency towards y.

∴ The non-resemblances observed are such as could not produce protective resemblances. This is a formally bad argument from two negative premisses justified by its positive meaning, which implies that *just where* the alleged effect ceases, the alleged cause ceases too.

If you look at the case in the Natural History Museum [1] you see the normal Pierinæ down one side, not approaching Euploinæ. They are the positive examples, negatively confirming the explanation of those which do approach Euploinæ. These latter all start from some form which varied slightly, by accident we presume, towards Euploinæ, and then this partially resembling series splits into three sets, each leading up to a different and complete protective resemblance.

I said *mere* number was no help in scientific Induction. But do not these three sets of resemblances make a stronger proof than any one would? Yes, because we need a presumption against accident. You would not want this if you could unveil what really happens in one case, but as infinite conditions are operative in such matters, and it is impossible to experiment accurately,[2] this cannot be done ;

---

[1] These cases in the entrance-hall of the Natural History Museum at South Kensington afford excellent practical illustrations of Inductive Method. I strongly urge the London student to try his hand at formulating them.

[2] Ultimately, no experiments are absolutely accurate. There is

and it might be said that *one* such resemblance was an accident, *i. e.* that it was owing to causes independent of the protection. But as the cases become more numerous it becomes more improbable that different circumstances produce the same effect, which would then be a mere coincidence, in so many different cases. If, however, we knew by positive and negative analysis what circumstance did produce the effect, this confirmation would be useless.

Negative
Instance.

(*f*) In order to show *exactly* what circumstance produces a given effect, a system must be brought to bear on the phenomenon through negation. The only test of truth is that it is that which enables you to organise your thought and perception.

The first means of doing this is Observation, then Experiment, then Classification and Hypothesis, which takes us into Deduction.

Observation is inaccurate, until you begin to distinguish what is connected from what is not connected. When you do this, you are very near experiment, the use of which is to introduce perfectly definite and measurable changes into what you are observing.[1] There is no absolute distinction between observation and experiment. Looking at a tissue through a microscope is observation ; putting on a polari-scope, though it changes the *image* altogether, is observation ; if you warm the stage, or put an acid on the object, that, I suppose, is experiment, because you interfere with the object

always an unexhausted background in which unsuspected causes of error may be latent.

[1] Jevons, *loc. cit.*, esp. quot. from Herschel (p. 234).

itself. What should we say, for example, as to spectroscopic analysis of the Sun's corona ?

The moment you begin accurate observation you get a negative with positive value, which is really the converse by negation of your positive observation. a_1 is b_1 ; b_2 (which is *just* not-b_1) is a_2 (which is *just* not-a_1). Thus the two may be represented as the same judgment in positive and negative forms, which confirm one another. " Yellow is a compound of red and green "—in Experiment, " if, and as far as you take away the red or the green you destroy the yellow." That describes an experiment with the colour-box. I have inverted the order in the conversions in compliance with the rule of common Logic, that Predicate is wider than Subject ; but in accurate matter it is a false rule, and very inconvenient. The common rule means that a man who is drowned is dead, but a man who is dead need not have been drowned ; but of course if he has the signs of death by drowning then he has been drowned.

(*g*) *Classification* is a consequence of all systematic theory ; it is not a separate method of science. It is merely the arrangement of positive contents negatively related. No doubt where we have a kind of family relations between individuals classification is more prominent, and in the theory of continuous matter or operation, where individualities are not remarkable—*e. g.* in geometry—it is less prominent. But both are always there—classification and theory. Classification which expresses no theory is worthless, except that intended for convenient reference, such as alphabetical classification.

Under classification I may say a word on generalisation.

Classification and Generalisation.

The common idea of inference from many cases, because they are many, to all cases of the same kind, is quite without justification. The only genuine and fundamental law of generalisation is "Once true always true." But this might fail to suffice for our practical purposes, because it might save its truth by abstraction. Let us take the example, "Water is made of oxygen and hydrogen." If that is true once, it is always true *in the same sense.* If you find some fluid of a different composition which you are inclined to call water, then you must identify or distinguish the two, and this is a mere question of classification. *Practically,* however, we could not get on unless our knowledge had some degree of *exhaustiveness, i. e.* unless we knew roughly that most of *what we take for water* will have the alleged properties. But no Induction or analysis, however accurate, can assure us against confusion and error, viz. assure us that everything we take to be water will be made of oxygen and hydrogen, nor that water will always be found on the earth. I call this accurate analysis, which *may* be made in a single instance only, and is the only perfectly scientific generalisation, generalisation by mere determination. Its classification is hypothetical, *i. e.* in it the individuals are merely possible individuals.

But this passes into another kind of generalisation, which may be called generalisation by concrete system, as when we attach scientific analysis to some extensive individual reality, *e. g.* to the solar system or the race of man. Then our judgments have a place in the real world, and our classification is categorical classification. The generalisation in this case does not follow from the judgment being extended

over a great plurality of possible similar subjects, but from
the subject to which it applies having as an organised totality
a large place in the world ; *e. g.* " The human race alone
gives moral interest to the history of our planet." These
judgments come by making explicit the reality which under-
lies such hypothetical judgments as "all men are capable
of morality." It means that we actually venture to assign
a place in the universe to the system we are speaking of.
Then, though it is an individual, and unique, its name has
a meaning, and is not a mere proper name. The solar
system is good instance. Judgments about it or parts of
it are universal but not purely hypothetical, and as our
knowledge of this kind increases it becomes even a little
exhaustive.

Generalisation by mere likeness or analogy, on the other
hand, is precarious. It is what popular theory has in its
mind in speaking of Induction, viz. a conclusion from a
truth to judgments concerning all similar cases, *e. g.* from
" Water is made of Oxygen and Hydrogen " to " All liquids
which we choose to take for water are made of Oxygen and
Hydrogen." No scientific method can possibly give us this
result. In as far as it has value it depends upon our guess-
ing rightly by analogy. It may be replied, "that the signs
of recognition are set down in the law or truth." Well, if
they are certain, generalisation by mere determination is
enough ; if they are doubtful, no induction can warrant your
judgment of them in particular cases. Practically, of course,
we get them right pretty often, although wrong very often. .

(*h*) Hypothesis is merely supposition ; it consists in sug- Hypo
gesting a fact as if it were real, when it is the only way of thesis.

M

completing given facts into a consistent system. If the hypothesis is proved that is a demonstration. It has been said that "Facts are only familiar theories." If a bell rings in the house, I say unhesitatingly, "Some one rang that bell." Once in ten years it may be rung, not by a person, but by some mechanical accident, in which case the "some one" is a hypothesis, but one always treats it as a fact. The only proof of a hypothesis is its being the only one that will fit the facts, *i. e.* make our system of reality relatively self-consistent. We believe many things we can *never* verify by perception, *e. g.* the existence of the centre of the earth, or that you have an idea in your minds; and if we go to ultimate analysis, perception itself involves hypothesis, and *a fortiori* all experiment involves hypothesis. Every experimental interference with nature involves some supposition as to a possible connection which it is intended to confirm or disprove.

Deduction.

2. Classification and hypothesis bring us into Deduction, which is not really a separate kind of inference from Induction, but is a name given to science when it becomes systematic, so that it goes from the whole to the parts, and not from the parts to the whole. In Induction you are finding out the system piecemeal, in Deduction you already have the clue; but the system, and the system only, is the ground of inference in both. Induction is tentative because we do not know the system completely. Their relation may be fairly represented by the relation of the first figure of the Syllogism to the second and third. The difference is merely that in deduction we are sure of having knowledge which covers the whole system. If a man observed, "The differ-

ence between the dark blood in the veins and the bright blood in the arteries calls for explanation," that is the beginning of Induction. If a man states the circulation of the blood as an explanation, that is Deduction. Really Induction is only a popular name for such Inference as deals with numbers of instances. Mill's experimental methods do not depend upon number of instances, but only upon content; they presuppose the instances already broken up into conditions A, B, C, and consequents a, b, c.

I must distinguish subsumption and construction as two forms of deduction. Only the former *properly* employs Syllogism in the first figure.

(*a*) Subsumption is argument by subject and attribute; Subsump-
i. e. when we do not know the system so as to construct the tion.
detail,—*e. g.* a man's character,—and can only state *in* what individual system the details occur. Then we *really want* the major premise to lay down the properties of the system, and all deduction *can* therefore be employed with a major premise, *e. g.* a mathematical argument might ultimately take the form, "*space is such that* two parallels cannot meet."

But (*b*) when the nature of the subject is very obvious, Construc
and the combinations in it very definite, then the major tion.
premise is superfluous, and adds nothing to the elements of the combination.

"A to right of B, B to right of C.

. · . A to right of C."

This is clear, but it is not formal; as a syllogism it has four terms. It is simply a construction in a series of which the nature is obvious. And if you insert a major premise it would be, "What is to the right of anything is to the right of that which the former is to the right of," and that is simply the nature of the series implied in the inference stated in an abstract form. "Inference is a construction followed by an intuition."[1] The construction, I think, however, must be a stage of the intuition. I am therefore inclined to suggest that a factor of general insight into principle is neglected in this definition, from which much may undoubtedly be learned.

Causation. 3. I have said very little about causation. The fact is, that in Logic the cause necessarily fades away into the reason, that is, the explanation. If we follow Mill's account, we see how this takes place. I will put the stages very briefly.

Cause. (*a*) We start, no doubt, by thinking of a cause as a real event in time, the priority of which is the condition of another event, the effect. Pull the trigger—cause—and the gun goes off—effect.

Complete conditions. (*b*) The moment we look closer at it, we see that this will not do, and we begin to say with Mill, that the cause is the antecedent which includes *all* the conditions of the effect. The plurality of alternative causes breaks down, through the conditions defining the effect. Pull the trigger?—yes, but the cartridge must be in its place, the striker must be straight, the cap must be in order, the powder must be dry and chemically fit, and so on, and so on, till it becomes pretty clear that the cause is a system of circumstances which include the effect.

Law. (*c*) But then our troubles are not ended. Only the essential and invariable conditions enter into the cause, if the

---

[1] Bradley, *Principles of Logic*, p. 235.

cause is invariable. This begins to cut away the particular circumstances of the case. You need not use the trigger, nor even the cap; you may ignite powder in many ways. You may have many kinds of explosives. All that is essential is to have an explosion of a certain force and not too great rapidity. Then you will get this paradox. What is merely essential to the effect, is always something less than any combination of real "things" which will produce the effect, because every real thing has many properties irrelevant to this particular effect. So, *if the cause means something real*, as a material object is real, it cannot be invariable and essential. If it is not something real, and is essential, it fines down into a reason or law—the antecedent in a hypothetical judgment.

(*d*) We can only escape this by identifying both cause and reason with the complete ground; that is, the nature of a system of reality within which the cause and effect both lie. But even then, though the ground is *real*, it is not antecedent in time. We see, indeed, that the conditions of an effect must be continuous through the effect. If the process were taken as cut in two at any point, its connection would be destroyed. If *a* cause and *b* effect were really detached events, what difference could it make if, instead of *a*, *c* preceded *b*? *Ground, or real system with known laws.*

4. The postulate of Knowledge, then, is very badly stated as Uniformity of Nature. That was due to the vulgar notion of Inductive "generalisation." It must be stated in two parts: first, "Once true always true;" and secondly, "Our truth is enough for us," that is, it covers enough of the universe for our practical and theoretical needs. The *Postulate of Knowledge.*

two parts may be put together by saying, "The universe is a rational system," taking rational to mean not only of such a nature that it can be known by intelligence, but further of such a nature that it can be known and handled by *our* intelligence.

Con-
clusion.

5. These lectures have been unavoidably descriptive rather than thorough, and yet, as I warned you, descriptive of properties which are in a sense not at all new, but quite familiar, and even trite. You will not feel, at first, that the full interest which I claimed for the science of knowledge, really attaches to these dry relations of abstract thought. You will get no permanent good unless you carry the study forward for yourselves, and use these ideas as a clue to find your bearings in the great world of knowledge.

And I would give you one hint about this. *I* do not suggest that you should neglect philosophy but yet you should remember that philosophy can tell you no new facts, and can make no discoveries. All that it can tell you is the significant connection of what you already know. And if you know little or nothing, philosophy has little or nothing to tell you. Plato says, "The synoptical man, the man who has a conspectus of knowledge, is the philosopher; and the man who is not synoptical, who cannot see two subjects in their relation, is no philosopher." By all means read good logical books; but also and more especially read good and thorough systematic books on science, or history, or politics, or fine art—I do not mean on all of these subjects, but on some, wherever your interest leads you. You cannot learn the nature of inference, of systematic necessity, of the construction of reality, by reading logic exclusively; you must feel it and possess it by working in the world of concrete knowledge. I give one example in passing. If you study social questions, test for yourselves the value of statistics— *i. e.* sets of enumerative judgments. Consider what the causal analysis of any problem demands; remember that all enumeration implies a ground or whole, on which its value depends; and contrast the exhaustive examination of an instance thoroughly known, with the enumeration of thousands of cases lumped under a general predicate. Determine always to know the truth; welcome all information and all suggestion, but remember that truth is always systematic, and that every judgment, when you scrutinise it, demands a fuller and fuller connection with the structure of life. It is not cleverness or learning that makes the philosopher; it is a certain spirit; openness of mind, thoroughness of work, and hatred of superficiality. Each of us, whatever his opportunities, can become in a true sense, if he has the real philosophic spirit, in Plato's magnificent words, "The spectator of all time and of all existence."

THE END

PRINTED IN GREAT BRITAIN BY
RICHARD CLAY AND COMPANY, LTD.,
BUNGAY, SUFFOLK